MONUMENT AVENUE Memories

GROWING UP ON RICHMOND'S GRAND AVENUE

Edited by *Patricia Cecil Hass*

THE
History
PRESS

Published by The History Press
Charleston, SC 29403
www.historypress.net

Copyright © 2013 by Patricia Cecil Hass
All rights reserved

First published 2013

ISBN 9781540208477

Library of Congress CIP data applied for.

Notice: The information in this book is true and complete to the best of our knowledge. It is offered without guarantee on the part of the author or The History Press. The author and The History Press disclaim all liability in connection with the use of this book.

CONTENTS

Foreword, by Margaret Page Bemiss   5

FitzGerald Bemiss   17
William Maury Hill   21
Archer Christian Burke   27
Hobson Goddin   37
Louise Brander Bunnell Nemecek   41
Anne Willson Harrison Eastman   47
John Howe Cecil Jr.   51
Patricia Cary Cecil Hass   57
Jane Abert Cecil   65
Gertrude Skelton Bryan   73
Roberta Bryan Bocock   83
Henry Harrison Wilson Jr.   97

Epilogue: Coleman Wortham III   99
Appendix   103
Notes on Sources   111
About the Editor   112

To the friends who worked in our families' houses and who made it all possible; for their unfailing patience, kindness, humor and their forbearance, we will always be grateful. With love, we dedicate this book to them.

FOREWORD

The history of Monument Avenue is the story of Richmond's transition from the nineteenth to the twentieth centuries and, as such, is a study in contradictions. Planned, or at least sold to the public, in 1887 as the backdrop for an equestrian statue of General Lee that had been stuck in a contentious site and design process for seventeen years, Monument Avenue was a hymn to the Lost Cause. With the later additions of J.E.B. Stuart and Jefferson Davis, four days apart in 1907, and Stonewall Jackson in 1919, its purpose was cast in bronze.

But as a grand, tree-lined residential boulevard, laid out by a young Harvard-educated engineer and planner, Collinson Pierrepont Edwards Burgwyn, it was a proclamation that Richmond had risen from its ashes of defeat and was open for national and international business. Richmond's Monument Avenue was to be ranked with Boston's Commonwealth, Cleveland's Euclid, New York's Fifth and Chicago's Prairie Avenues as a place for elegant mansions of the wealthy and successful. With it, Richmond was claiming a place in the City Beautiful movement of the post–Civil War Gilded Age.

Monument Avenue, like Richmond's earlier residential neighborhoods to the east, beginning with Church Hill, was also a development scheme: one that required annexing 292 acres of land across the Henrico line that mostly belonged to three families: Allen, Branch and Sheppard. This had the further advantage, stated openly by Governor FitzHugh Lee, of enlarging the city's tax base, but the politics were complicated. Funds for the Lee statue had been solicited and raised far outside Richmond, and some of the donors complained that their money should not be used to improve the finances of the city of Richmond. It was not until 1892 that Governor Lee was able to push the annexation through the legislature.

The saga of the Lee statue began in 1870, after Lee's death, when two rival groups set themselves up to decide on a suitable memorial. One was made up of former Confederate officers led by General Jubal Early, and the other, the Ladies' Lee Monument Association, "was a group of patrician Richmond women led by Sarah Nicholas Randolph." Mrs. Randolph felt strongly that the statue, as well as being a faithful likeness of the great man, should be "great art." There was spirited discussion as to the location of a proposed statue. The first suggestion was Hollywood Cemetery, then Libby Hill and then Gamble's Hill, but no decision was reached.

The men's group floundered into disorganization almost immediately and was succeeded by a new men's group chartered by the General Assembly and led by the newly elected governor, James Kemper. In October 1877, this committee announced a competition for the design of a statue. The Ladies joined forces with this new group for a while but found working with the men discouraging and pulled out. The committee had no prize money, no certainty that a statue would be erected and an amateur jury whose members based their opinions on whether they considered the models to properly resemble General Lee and his horse, Traveller.

Edward Valentine, a Richmond sculptor who had recently finished the enormously popular *Recumbent Lee* at the newly christened Washington and Lee University in Lexington (formerly Washington College), won the most votes, but there were complaints that he hadn't got Traveller right. Moses Ezekiel, another Richmonder who had fought as a Virginia Military Institute (VMI) cadet at the Battle of New Market, sent an entry from Rome, but the jury didn't like his horse either. Another American living in Rome, A.E. Harnish, sent a model of Lee being led into Valhalla by Fame. The jury finally selected the entry of a self-taught female sculptor, Vinnie Ream, but somehow they never announced her as the winner. Then, when the models were put on exhibit at the state library, all the entries were panned, and the whole thing fizzled. The committee announced another competition the next year, but only got four entries and nothing came of it.

That was the end of that, until 1884, by which time a new governor had been elected. FitzHugh Lee was General Lee's nephew, and shortly after his election, he decreed a merger of the two committees, making it clear that it was time to get on with the statue of General Lee. Shortly thereafter, the Ladies group, which had been quietly going about its business under the radar, suddenly announced a new competition, with the cut-off date for entries set for February 1, 1886. Sarah Nicholas Randolph pronounced that the monument should be "art rather than fact." The group offered cash prizes, held an exhibition of the entries at the Corcoran Gallery in Washington and nominated a distinguished jury consisting of two eminent sculptors, Augustus Saint-Gaudens and John Quincy Adams Ward, as well as Edward Clark, architect of the U.S. Capitol. The announced winner was Charles Henry Niehaus, a young sculptor from Cincinnati, whose choice of site was a plaza on Gamble's Hill. Unfortunately, he showed Lee on a bobtailed, prancing horse, and Jubal Early threatened to "blow up the thing with dynamite" if it was erected. When that brouhaha died down, the jury quietly awarded the commission to an internationally recognized French sculptor, Marius-Jean-Antonin Mercié, who happened to be a friend and ex-roommate of Augustus Saint-Gaudens.

Somehow, somewhere along the way, a deal must have been struck between the Ladies and the governor: the group could choose the sculptor, and he could choose the site. The wily Ladies could see that having a sculptor of international renown would promote General Lee to the status of a "great military leader in the company of Alexander the Great, Caesar and Napoleon," as befitted a hero at the head of a great boulevard like those in Boston and New York. And the governor saw the chance to enlarge the city and its tax base; he therefore, also quietly, accepted the gift of an eleven-acre field, just outside the city limit, as a site for the proposed statue. The field belonged to Otway Allen and his three sisters, the heirs of William C. Allen, a successful developer who, starting out as a brick mason, amassed a good deal of property before his death in 1874. One of his holdings, bought as a long-term investment, was a fifty-eight-acre tract bordering the western edge of the city, reaching from Lombardy to present-day Allison Street, that he left to his four children. His son, Otway, also a shrewd businessman, parlayed his father's fortune into social and civic success as well. The younger Allen was a friend and political supporter of FitzHugh Lee, and the eleven acres that the Allens donated for the Lee monument were part of their father's legacy.

Otway Allen also had the foresight to commission the city engineer, C.P.E. Burgwyn, to draw up plans for a grand boulevard as a suitable background for the heroic statue. The field, most recently used as a baseball field, abutted the western end of Franklin Street at its intersection with Lombardy Street. This placement would align the statue of Lee on axis with the Capitol Square and, by association, link it to the Houdon statue of Washington inside the

Capitol, as well as the Rogers-Crawford equestrian statue of Washington and his cabinet. It would also tie Franklin Street, which had become Richmond's most fashionable residential street, to the new development, albeit with a new name.

Collinson Pierrepont Edwards Burgwyn, who designed the plan for Monument Avenue, was born in North Carolina and lived in Richmond as a child. He graduated from Harvard in 1874, received his engineering degree in 1876 and worked for one year in Cambridge before returning to Richmond in 1877. He worked first for the city, supervising improvements to the James River channel and working on the new city hall. At some point, he was engaged as a consultant by the Ladies Lee Monument Association. For Allen, he drew an elegant nine-block plan (now in the collection of the Valentine Museum) for the previously open land bounded by Lombardy Street, an alley between Park Avenue and the new boulevard, and Broad Street. It proposed cross-axial boulevards with a fifty-foot median and a two-hundred-foot circle at the intersection of Allen Avenue and Franklin Street for the Lee monument. The plan ended at a proposed but then unnamed cross street one block west of Meadow Street.

There were a few more chapters to the story, resulting in the statue's being enlarged from thirteen to twenty-one feet in height and the pedestal from thirty-five to forty so that General Lee would tower over the city, standing taller than George Washington in the Rogers-Crawford statue in Capitol Square.

On October 27, 1887, the cornerstone for the Lee monument was dedicated. A parade of former Confederate soldiers marched up from Capitol Square and stood in a raw, cold rain to hear Governor Lee introduce the proceedings. Dr. Moses D. Hoge, minister of the Second Presbyterian Church, gave a dedicatory prayer, and Charles Marshall, Lee's military secretary, provided an oration. There were still complaints about the site, but it was too late, and two and a half years later, on May 4, 1890, four crates containing the pieces of the Lee statue that had been shipped from France to New York, and thence by rail to Richmond, arrived at the station at Eighth and Broad Streets.

In an organized parade, between ten and twenty thousand Richmonders took turns hauling the crates up Broad Street to Lombardy and then south to the erstwhile baseball field. When the parade reached its destination, the hauling ropes were cut into pieces, tied with ribbon and given as souvenirs to the families of the haulers, who "saved the scraps and passed them on for generations."

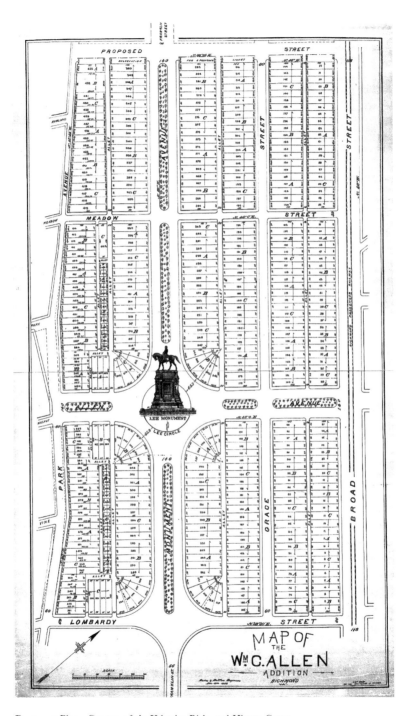

Burgwyn Plan. *Courtesy of the Valentine Richmond History Center.*

Monument Avenue with newly planted trees, 1904. *Courtesy of the Valentine Richmond History Center.*

It took three weeks to assemble all the parts of the long-awaited statue, a process followed closely by the citizenry. Finally, on May 29, 1890, the Lee monument was unveiled to great fanfare, and Monument Avenue was officially born.

Development along the new avenue was slow at first, largely due to the Panic of 1893. By 1894, only one house had been built, 1601 Monument Avenue, by Otway Warwick, of Warwick Brothers Tobacco Supplies. (The house was demolished in 1978). In 1901, curbs and gutters were laid as far as Meadow Street. In 1904, trees went in, scarlet and sugar maples in single rows along the new sidewalks and a double row in the median. It took Otway Allen several years to decide to build on his new avenue, and he died in 1911 before the completion of his Colonial Revival mansion at 1611, designed by Claude K. Howell. His widow moved into it, and her sister and brother-in-law built next door. One of the Allen sisters, Martha Allen Wise, employed Isaac T. Skinner to design a house at 1808 Monument, a family pattern that was quite often repeated as development grew westward and which partly accounts for the sense of neighborhood on each block of the new avenue.

After the turn of the century, as development progressed, the cross street west of Meadow became Allison Street, named for James W. Allison, who, with his partner Edmund B. Addison, owned the land that became the 2200 block of Monument Avenue, bracketed by Allison and Addison

Monument Avenue looking east from Stonewall Jackson monument at the Boulevard. *Courtesy of the Valentine Richmond History Center.*

Streets. Their block developed a little differently, starting at the west end of the block and filling in to the east, from 1908 to 1918. There was also a greater variety of sizes and building styles than there had been on most of the blocks of the Allen property. The buildings of the 2200 block ran the gamut from large, single-family dwellings to smaller-spec houses, as well as the second and third apartment buildings on Monument: the Addison apartments at number 2226 in 1910 and the Brooke Apartments at number 2225 in 1912. (The first apartment building on Monument was the Stafford, built at 2007 Monument Avenue in 1909, one year before the Addison.) All three were architect-designed, elegant buildings, clearly meant to appeal to people who were used to elegance, and though there were single-family zoning regulations in place at the time, nobody bothered to enforce them.

West of the Allens' fifty-eight acres and the one-block-long parcel owned by James Allison and Edmund Addison, Patteson Branch had bought in the 1880s a large tract of more than two hundred acres in Henrico, stretching from what became Addison (now Strawberry) Street to the Boulevard and from Park Avenue to Broad Street. He transferred most of it to the Kingsland

South side of the 2300 block of Monument, under construction. *Courtesy of the Valentine Richmond History Center.*

Land Company, run by his son, John Kerr Branch, and his nephew, Robert G. Cabell. In 1907, the dedication of the Jefferson Davis monument at the west end of the 2300 block of Monument Avenue provoked an immediate spread of development in that direction, and the 2300 block became the site of some of the grandest houses on the avenue. Because the Branch property was divided into irregular and larger lots, the southern side of the 2300 block has a very different feel from the rest of Monument Avenue.

Between 1917 and 1919, John Kerr Branch built by far the largest, most impressive and most expensive house on Monument Avenue at number 2501, designed by John Russell Pope. Two nephews and two great-nephews built nearby, and another neighborhood was established.

The development of Monument Avenue between Lombardy and the Boulevard was driven not just by successful members of Richmond's old Protestant families building their grand new houses on a fashionable street; Richmond's Jewish community also had a large presence. Temple Beth Ahabah, one block down from St. James on Franklin Street, was the sixth-oldest Jewish congregation in America. Bankers, lawyers and doctors joined

Interior of 2304 Monument Avenue. *Courtesy of the Valentine Richmond History Center.*

newly prosperous real estate developers, contractors, civil engineers, lumber and oil merchants and the officers of the Binswanger Glass Company. All recognized the advantages of Monument Avenue as a showroom for their products and their talents. Many of the earlier developers and builders

Branch House. *Courtesy of the Valentine Richmond History Center.*

themselves designed the houses they built, but a clutch of favored architects included Carneal and Johnson, Claude K. Howell, Noland and Baskervill, Isaac T. Skinner and, later, William Lawrence Bottomley and Duncan Lee.

The third family whose land became part of the Monument Avenue development was the Sheppard family. The Sheppards came from Buckingham County, and in the 1870s, John Sheppard bought land in Henrico as an investment. He never lived in Richmond, but he was involved in land speculation with his brother, Nicholas, who did have a farmhouse on the property, and with Major James C. Dooley, who lived at Maymont. The pattern of development on the Sheppard tract, from the Boulevard west to Roseneath, was quite different from the eastern part of Monument, where great houses held sway. Large apartment houses sprang up cheek by jowl, along with smaller, more modest ones, as well as, every now and then, a big house like those east of the Boulevard. All of these were built after 1912, and most of them after the First World War.

When Monument Avenue was extended in the 1920s to include the Sheppard property, large apartment buildings were the rule, not the exception, and the tradition of beautiful buildings was largely upheld. However, when development after the Second World War continued Monument Avenue's westward march all the way to Glenside Drive, economic reality as well as modern building styles decreed that a very different kind of building took over, and past the railroad tracks, the unusual continuity and architectural character of Monument Avenue was lost.

The statue of Stonewall Jackson, at the intersection of Monument Avenue and the Boulevard, was dedicated in 1919. Although his monument had been in the planning since 1915, it was not until 1929 that Matthew Fontaine Maury, "Pathfinder of the Seas," came to the intersection of Monument and Belmont. The last statue to be built on Monument Avenue was that of Arthur Ashe, which was dedicated on July 10, 1996, at the intersection of Monument and Roseneath. It caused enormous controversy, but whatever one may think of its placement or its artistic merit, it is a fitting symbol. Continuing to honor its heroes, Richmond is moving on. The process is still not complete, but we have entered the twenty-first century.

The storytellers whose memories make up this book grew up and played on the blocks of Monument between General Lee and Jefferson Davis. One of them, Gerry Bemiss, lived at 1811 Monument Avenue, built in 1904 for George J. Freedley and bought by the Bemisses in 1925. Following a time-honored Monument Avenue tradition, it was right across the street from his grandparents' house at number 1812, built by Louis W. Pizzini in 1904 and sold to DeSoto FitzGerald when he moved from Savannah to Richmond that same year. Gerry loved Monument Avenue and its history. He loved telling stories, and he once put together a collection of his favorites, which included this one about Mrs. John Kerr Branch, who lived in the Branch House at 2501 Monument Avenue between sojourns in Italy and Pawling, New York:

> *Stories don't have to stick to the facts. Facts can be used if they are helpful, but certainly should not be allowed to hamper a story. Lowell Thomas became rich and famous telling stories quite detached from the facts. He encountered T.E. Lawrence, named him Lawrence of Arabia, and made him a world celebrity, crediting him with leadership of the Arab revolt far beyond his real role.*
>
> *I met Lowell Thomas at a political convention in Chicago. He learned that I was from Richmond and asked me if I knew Mrs. Branch. She was a wealthy old lady, a friend of my grandparents, who spent several months each year in Pawling, N.Y. where Mr. Thomas lived. He said, "Let me tell you a remarkable story about her. She lived in a grand house in Fiesole (near Florence) and one night a burglar climbed through her bedroom window,*

held a knife at her throat and said, 'Your jewels or your neck.' Mrs. Branch wisely produced the jewels, and the burglar fled with them.

Next morning, in a temper, she set about getting Mussolini on the phone, which she had just enough prominence and brass to accomplish. She told Il Duce what had happened to her, scolded him roundly and demanded that he do something about it. Il Duce said that he in no way condoned this sort of behaviour, and that she would hear from him within twenty-four hours. Sure enough, early next morning a messenger appeared at Mrs. Branch's front door and returned the jewels."

When I returned to Richmond, I soon encountered John Rennolds, Mrs. Branch's grandson, to whom I told Mr. Thomas' story. John responded, "Mr. Thomas loves that story and tells it all the time. I can assure you that there is not a word of truth in it."

MARGARET PAGE BEMISS
January 2013

FitzGerald Bemiss

W hen we were young, Monument Avenue was a lovely place to live. Children and grownups moved about the city freely. Traffic and crime were not problems. I recall my father hanging a kerosene lantern on the left rear bumper of his Chevrolet; in those days, it was not rare that an object of this sort be left on the street overnight. We spent hours and hours roller skating and bicycling wherever curiosity took us. West Avenue was the only street smoothly paved and suitable for stick games on skates, but you, a Monument Avenue person, were an outsider and a trespasser, so we had to tread lightly.

These were the days before suburbia, and it seemed that *everyone* lived in the city. My parent's friends lived in the immediate neighborhood, and their children tended to be our playmates and friends. I can still name several families on each of the nearby blocks. I also recall an elderly lady steering her electric car down the avenue with a tiller. She had a small flower vase on the interior of each side.

Most of the deliveries were by horse and wagon. At various points around town, there were handsome stone watering troughs for a still largely horse-drawn community. The *clop-clop* of the iceman's and the milkman's horses in the early morning skirting Lee's monument just below my window was reassuring. Another sound that indicated that all was right was Sheppard's (our butler) broom sweeping the torrent of the glorious autumn mixture of yellow, red and brown leaves off our sidewalk.

Monument Avenue would be a splendid thing in any league, starting at Capitol Square and calling itself Franklin Street until it reaches Lombardy

Gerry and Cynthia in front of a fire at 1811. *Courtesy of Margaret Bemiss.*

for the rest of its five-mile length as Monument Avenue. The handsomest section is between General J.E.B. Stuart at Lombardy, where the green median and the separate east- and westbound lanes and the ample sidewalks provide enough space for four maple trees abreast. St. James's Church is on the block east of Lombardy, and its spire, a beautiful one backstanding General Lee, delights me every time I see it. The grand section of the avenue ends at General Stonewall Jackson's monument on the Boulevard. A stroll down the median from Jackson to Stuart is an hour very well spent.

Most of the houses had front porches. In the cool of the evening, people would come out and sit a while. West Avenue used to regard the street as its living room, where all the chitchat took place. The houses were simply places to park temporarily until everyone felt they just had to join their friends in the street. But on Monument Avenue, the real reason for a front porch

Opposite, top: Lee, with St. James spire. *Courtesy of the Richmond History Center.*

Opposite, bottom: Churchill and Eisenhower riding in a carriage in a parade on Monument Avenue on March 8, 1946. *Courtesy of the Valentine Richmond History Center.*

Senator FitzGerald Bemiss, 1960. *Courtesy of Margaret Bemiss.*

was for watching parades. Usually they started at the Boulevard and came down Monument, often ending up at Hollywood Cemetery. The best, of course, were Ringling Brothers Barnum & Bailey, with elephants, lions, tigers, clowns—indeed, the whole works. There were other good parades with ancient Civil War veterans and Richmond Blues in their dashing uniforms.

The more I thought about the Ten Commandments, the more I felt I recognized them and had seen them in action. They were, of all things, the foundation of my childhood home on Monument Avenue. They fitted perfectly. What the critics say is missing in sprawling suburbia—sense of place, amenities and, yes, beauty—is abundant in the city, and after a brief period in the '50s, when so many people moved out, there began a trickle of people moving back to the city for a more interesting life. That has now become a substantial flow. Certainly there are problems in the city, but remember what Mark Twain said: "Heaven for climate, Hell for company."

WILLIAM MAURY HILL

My father, Julien Harrison Hill, built our house in about 1903, and it was called the Hill House, not the Maury House, as some believe. I lived at 1810 Monument Avenue, right across the street from FitzGerald Bemiss and right next door to Mr. FitzGerald. And right next to General Lee's statue, which I used to salute every morning when I got out of bed. We were very connected to General Lee. In fact, my sister Diana, had the same birthday, January 19. On that date, there was always a parade up and down Monument Avenue, and when she was little, she thought that parade was in her honor!

My friends in those days were Mason Williams and Morrison Hutcheson. The Williamses lived on Park Avenue, right across on the corner of Park and Allen. The Hutchesons lived down on Park a little bit. And, of course, I played with Andy Christian when his family moved to 1820 Monument. As boys, we all used to play up and down Monument Avenue on the grassplots, and the police would come and chase us off 'cause they didn't like us playing there. We would see them coming, and we would run and hide in the backyard. We were scared they would put us in jail. Even so, when they were gone, we would go right back out to the grassplot and keep playing. We were also scared of the West Avenue gang; when they came over, we ran. We were afraid of them because they were very tough.

I cannot remember the lady's name who later built two houses just toward Allen Avenue from us, but earlier, that had also been a vacant lot. And right across the street, next to the Bemisses, there also was a vacant lot. We used to play on that vacant lot all the time, mostly playing ball. One day, we hit a ball, and it went in the third-floor window and landed in Cynthia's crib. Mr. Bemiss did not like that, and he called up to give us a hard time, and Mason went *psssss* and hung up. Mr. Bemiss then invited us to come over there and gave us ice cream. I think he thought being courteous was better than blessing us out, because it made us ashamed.

Still, we did all kinds of mischievous things that boys do. For example, St. James Church is just about two blocks away, and one day, Mason Williams and I put Armistead, his little brother, who was probably five or six, up on the roof next door to St. James's and left. I have no idea how he got down. We also used to jump from roof to roof on Park Avenue. We couldn't do it on Monument Avenue because the houses were too far apart. When it snowed, we would get up on the grassplot and slide down a little bit, but mostly we would catch on to the bumpers of cars and get them to pull us on our sleds.

My two older sisters, Anne and Diana, had horses at the Hunt Club that was out on Broad Street, on Staples Mill Road. In those days, the railroad tracks went right across Monument Avenue on the Acca Bridge, and the Deep Run Hunt Club was right there. I rode as well, and in fact, right next door to 1810, there was a vacant lot belonging to the Antrims, where for a while my family kept a horse or a pony for me in our backyard, and I would take it out to graze in that lot right next door. Later, we used to bring our horses over and ride them up and down Monument Avenue. At that time, past Westmoreland Street, Monument Avenue was only one lane, but there was a dirt road beside the paved road that was nice and flat. We could just dash all the way from Westmoreland Street west to the end at Horsepen Road.

In the 1920s and '30s, there were many parades on the avenue. There was always a parade on General Lee's birthday on January 19. Most parades started at the Boulevard or at the Davis monument, came down the avenue all the way down to Laurel Street and ended up at historic Hollywood Cemetery.

As members of our family, we had Rosa and Luther Waytes, our cook and butler, and Emmett Crump, our laundress and seamstress. Emmett became the cook after Luther and Rosa moved to Charlottesville. Emmett's father, a white man, was the landlord who had two little girls, Emmett and Martha, the latter of whom became a schoolteacher. He always took care of the children. The girls and their mother had a very pretty house in Jackson Ward that was demolished when the expressway was built. Julia Cook came when Emmett moved to a nursing home.

Billy Hill with his pony in the vacant lot next door to 1810. *Courtesy of William M. Hill.*

Billy Hill and friends at the Deep Run Hunt Club on Broad Street at Westmoreland. *Back row, left to right*: Maria Gray Valentine, Diana Hill, Jackie Bryan, Jimmie Morgan, Freddie Campbell and Anne Hill. *Front row, left to right*: unknown, Libby Christian, William M. Hill, Elizabeth Leake, Frances Sampson and Tommy Cauthorne. *Courtesy of William M. Hill.*

When Emmett died, she left a large amount of money to a host of good friends and to her church. When she retired, she asked us to meet her at her bank, and she gave $1,000 to me, $500 to my wife, Ruth, and $100 to each of our four children. She didn't want us to tell anyone in the black community about this gift.

My father was considered the best-looking gentleman in Richmond. When he walked by the Collegiate School, down on the next block from us, all the girls rushed to the window to see him. When I was sixteen, he gave me a convertible with a rumble seat. I took Andy Christian to school and stopped farther up the avenue to pick up Morty Thalhimer and Henry Stern as well. They all took turns riding in the rumble seat.

My sister Lucy was very beautiful. In fact, all of my six older sisters were pretty. When Lucy was only seventeen, she met a very handsome Brazilian prince at Cape May, where our family went in the summer and where I was born. The prince was the grandson of Simón Bolívar. He fell madly in love with Lucy and wanted to marry her. Our parents were not interested in her getting married then.

When Lucy was twenty-four, she entered a convent in France called the Servants of the Blessed Sacrament. This was a very cloistered order. She wore her aunt's fur coat for the journey across the ocean. She never left the convent—a real story of true renunciation. She always seemed happy in her letters to us and on our visits to see her. The first time my wife, Ruth, ever met Lucy, back in the early '60s, she was seated behind a grated window in the convent in Paris.

On another visit with our children, the boys had fun throwing the football to the nuns at the convent in Lyon, where Lucy had been moved. We all went to a chapel to see the bones of martyrs plastered in the walls of the chapel. Later, we realized we had lost the football. When we came home and developed the pictures, there was the football in a pew in the chapel. The nuns were thrilled.

During World War II, Lucy was interned by the Germans, but toward the end of the war, she was sent to Waterville, Maine, where there was another Order of the Blessed Sacraments. As the only American in the convent in Paris, the Germans sent her to Maine in exchange for German prisoners. She died in Lyon in 1994, age ninety. We saw her ten days before she died, as well as the place where she was buried.

Archer Christian Burke

I lived at 2020 Monument Avenue in the 1930s for about eight years, and I lived at number 1820 before that. I have wonderful memories, and one of the things that strikes me now as I look back is how free we were to run around. Our parents never asked us where we were going or when we were coming back, and we roamed all over the "Fan." For example, a friend and I, clutching our nickels, would cross alleys and Grace Street to get to the Health Center Bowling Alley on the other side of Broad Street. I remember the grubby-looking men who were always hanging around in there, but we paid them no attention and they never bothered us.

Often we would walk up to the Capitol Theatre and see Sonja Henie or Shirley Temple movies, and then we would come home and put on our roller skates and pretend like we were ice skating if it was Sonja or put on our tap shoes if it was Shirley. On Saturday mornings, we would walk to the Byrd Theater to see the westerns, and I don't remember having any trouble or anybody speaking to us or anything like that. Then we would wander down on West Avenue to see the boys playing street hockey.

Before I gained independence, I remember walking with "Mammy" when I was about three, flinging a tantrum and falling limp on the sidewalk in front of Mrs. Davidson's and Mrs. Gwathmey's house on the north side of the 1600 block of Monument Avenue. No persuading would quiet me and my thrashing. I was too tired to walk home. Mammy was mortified over my behavior. The two sisters came calmly down to the sidewalk carrying a box

Jean Cunningham (Salley), Archer Christian (Burke) and Martha Lafferty (Burnett), 1930s.
Courtesy of Archer Christian Burke.

of Madame Eva's. I stuffed two in my mouth, stood up quietly and off I went toward home. I always loved them. (The ladies, that is.)

Mammy (Ella Fountain) slept on a cot at the foot of my bed until she left when I started school. She was a lovely, gray-haired, fulsome woman whom I adored and saw more of than my mother. It was very traumatic when she left. Every lonely night, I was terrified that the Lindbergh killer would kidnap me. After many long nightly sessions, my exasperated mother finally said to me, very sternly, "Who in the world would want to kidnap you?" Of course! End of problem!

I seemed to be the boss of the little girls who played in the grassplot, but only when Mary Anne Harrison was not there. When she appeared, the world stopped and waited for her directions. Before she moved to Connecticut at an early age, she lived at 2020 Monument before my family. After finishing Vassar College, she married John Lindsay, who later became mayor of New York City. We had many mutual friends in "the North" and remained close until she died some years ago. She was very attractive and maintained her "presence" throughout her life.

As children, we were never bored. We knew who lived in most of the houses from J.E.B. Stuart's monument to Stonewall Jackson's monument. We always had plans for the next day, very simple ones, but innocent and fun. Sometimes, on a rainy Sunday afternoon, Cynthia Bemiss would walk up to my house. We would get out an old blanket (our "holy" blanket, full of moth holes), spread it out on our staircase's second-floor landing and one of us would sit on it, wrap it around us and slip and slide furiously down to the bottom landing. We would laugh hysterically over the speed and lack of control. How did the rest of my family stand it? After a while, we would set up a card table on the landing, cover the table with the blanket and play house. Anyone who wanted to go up or down would have to use the back steps to the pantry. My parents had to have been out somewhere! It was a charmed life we led.

My family all went to St. Paul's Episcopal Church, except my Rennolds grandmother, who went to St. James's. Quite a few of my friends went there as well, so my family would drop me off at St. James's every Sunday on their way to St. Paul's. Afterward, Cynthia Bemiss and I would walk home with Anne Jackson, Jean Cunningham and others to play before Sunday dinner.

The 2300 block was probably more stylish than the 1800 and 2000 blocks. They had side walkways, but between our houses, we only had firm black dirt. But it was always damp and cool and shady in the summer. If a house cut in and became narrower, like Diana Hurt's, it would give us more available

Archer Christian (Burke), Betty Preston (Lottimore), Cynthia Bemiss (Stuart) and Maria Carter (Satterfield) in a fashion show. *Courtesy of Archer Christian Burke.*

black earth, where boys and girls would play mumbly peg or "territory" with a knife (throwing knives in a big circle to claim a slice).

Most houses had a full second floor, but the third floor was just a half floor. We would go to the second-floor roof, and the boys—Winkie McGeorge, probably, and others—would jump from the third floor of my house to the house next door.

On the other side was a three-floor apartment house. There was a grumpy woman who lived on the third floor, and she washed her sheets and hung them on a pulley to dry. One day, a little group of friends and I were waiting for her in my backyard. It was decided to throw mud on those sheets, so we got a lot of mud and just threw these mud cakes up on her sheets. All of a sudden, she came out ranting and raging and said she would call the police. My friends ran, and the police came and there I stood. I had not actually thrown the mud. It was the others' doing, but there I was, caught by the police. But what could they do with me, standing there crying and wailing? All they did was admonish me and leave.

Mary Jackson Shepherd (later, Shep Blair) always came up with the fun for the day. She loved to ask Billy Mann to come up and plays cars in her sandbox. Our miniature cars were old and rusty, and his were the latest models and brand new. Mary Jack would build tunnels and garages in the sand for his new tootsie toy cars and somehow "forget" where she put them. Billy would be frustrated at not being able to find them and would run home very upset. How she kept him coming back to play I don't know, especially as she continued to "lose" his new cars in the sand, as we watched this drama play out day after day with great fascination. I am sure eventually he retrieved them from Mary Jack's collection of shiny new cars.

I think the 2000 block of Monument Avenue had more children than any other single block. The ones I saw almost daily and knew quite well but have not mentioned because of no particular antics were Nancy Mann, John Newton Gray, the three Bunnell girls, Robert Hurt, the three Piper children, Anne Willson and Hawky Harrison and Margaret Anderton, a friend of my sister, Nelly. I think the two Bullock boys moved there after I left. Also Nan Hart (Stone) around the block on West Grace Street is still a good friend. I could go on and on because all of us in the Fan had a special bond that has lasted a lifetime. Interesting, we must have represented eight or ten schools, including Fox, Binford, St. Catherine's, St. Christopher's, Collegiate and Thomas Jefferson. Our school friends rarely mixed with our block pals—just an understood fact.

Our families all used the same businesses: R.L. Christian (groceries), Reuben's (Deli), Foys or Stuart Circle Pharmacy, the Capitol Theatre, Addison Cleaners, Pleasants Hardware, White's Restaurant (taffy lollipops!), the Woman's Exchange, the Health Center (bowling) and Sarah Lee Kitchen (bakery). Consequently, every household was similar, and we felt very comfortable visiting one another. We practically got the same food if we were staying at somebody's house for supper.

During all of our activities, certain aromas would fill the air. Richmond was a fairly small city in the 1930s, and the Southern Biscuit Company was about half a mile from my house, over past Broad Street and west of the Broad Street Station. If we had a breeze from the northwest, we knew what cookies they were baking for national consumption that day. The Sauer's Vanilla Company, again over on Broad Street, was even closer. Its huge neon sign, with moving people, lit up the sky at night and could be seen from my brother's third-floor bedroom. Duke's Mayonnaise and all sorts of spices are still made there today, but our favorite smell was the vanilla extract. The scent is still vivid in my mind, eighty years later. Often the scent of tobacco wafted from across the river. We felt we were luckier than some cities.

My parents' lives were so different. They were busy with my father's law firm; the Country Club of Virginia; the Woman's Club; the Commonwealth Club; the Bridge Club; the Book Club; Dr. Freeman's current events class; the Richmond German, hunting and fishing clubs; the Junior League; Sheltering Arms Hospital; and other charities, and they did not worry about their children. If we had a problem or needed help, we knew to run to the faithful, loving and intelligent keepers of our houses for consolation and solutions. I spent a lot of time in the kitchen, begging to do minor food preparations and listening to wonderful words of wisdom from Lelia and Nancy.

I got street smarts when I learned to ride the streetcar. A few years later, at my constant urging, our family finally moved to Westhampton. None of my friends knew about downtown, but I knew it all. On Saturdays, I would lead the group downtown on a streetcar to the record shop, White's for lunch and a movie at Loew's.

I was very close to my grandmother Rennolds, the one who went to St. James and lived at 2222 Monument. She had a huge midday dinner every day at her house, and any of her children, grandchildren or in-laws could just show up without notice. Usually there were at least eight of us at the dining room table. Lucy, her cook, was the best. It was where I learned to love turnip greens, "simlins," shad roe and anything that was a little unusual.

Marmee also had a little closet with a window under the steps in her house where she always kept a Whitman's Sampler box of candy and movie magazines. I never questioned why, but just lately I've realized they must have been put there for me. Several times a month, two or three friends and I would roller skate up to her house, go inside (skates on) and skate to the closet, unannounced. We would avail ourselves of candy and a magazine and leave. I never looked back at the floors for scratches.

Regularly, her chauffeur (Clark) would wrap her warmly with a robe in her big black Cadillac, deposit a hot brick on the floor of the back seat to warm her feet and drive to the spring at Byrd Park. I loved to go with them and hand the empty jugs to Clark to be filled with drinking water—a simple pleasure and a fond memory.

Another thing I have just realized while writing about my childhood is that it was no coincidence that this grandmother, Mrs. Robert Gordon Rennolds, lived on Monument Avenue between Allison and Addison Streets. Addison Street was named for her father (my great-grandfather, Edmund B. Addison) and Allison Street for his business partner, James W. Allison. Eventually, their company merged with Virginia Carolina Chemical Company.

At least once a year, the phone would really be buzzing. A childhood friend of my mother's, whom she used to visit at Mirador in Albemarle County, Nancy Lancaster, a niece of Lady Astor, would be coming to town from England, where she lived as an adult, and the calendar would be filling up with luncheons, teas and dinner parties. Gratefully, she took turns where she would stay so that she only visited us once in five or six years, but I remember entertaining at our house. She was full of personality, very good-looking and very kind and nice to her friends' children. I suspect that most men admired her also. I never had the opportunity of visiting her in England, but another Richmonder, Elizabeth Willard Herbert, and her children spent a lot of time with us and we with them at Teton House, Taunton (Somerset) in England. Her sister had married Kermit Roosevelt, and Elizabeth had married a knighted Englishman (for his work as an archaeologist in Egypt). Their father had been an ambassador to Spain. Once, upon leaving us, I went along to Byrd Airport to see them off. The airport was small, and that form of travel was still in its infancy. I will never forget this daring adventure of a mother and her children boarding this huge conveyance in the dark, where they were to get undressed, get into bunks and be flown to England. Her family owned the Willard Hotel in Washington and other businesses, so her children continued to come to the United States. Occasionally, they would stay with me after I was married. The first time, my contemporary, Mervyn, put his shoes outside his bedroom door at night. The next morning, he appeared in the kitchen as I was cooking breakfast, and I could not contain myself: "Who did you think was going to shine your shoes?!" I think he realized that our lifestyles were sadly different.

I also remember the following: the "X" marks painted on the curbs in front of the houses by beggars during the depression that identified these houses as providing good food; Mr. Winglinger, who delivered the *New York Times* to subscribers from his bicycle and collected his money once a week—he was a local character whom the boys called "Wing"; and Reuben's Delicatessen at Meadow and Park, where we took our ten cents' allowance and gazed at the huge display of penny candy to figure out how much we could get for a dime: bubble gum, Tootsie Rolls, Butterfingers, hard balls, Mary Janes or Baby Ruths. I remember the mysterious house on the northwest corner of the 2000 block of Monument Avenue. It was pristine, freshly painted and immaculate with the shades inside covering every window, and no one was ever seen coming or going. Our imaginations conjured up many stories, including spies and thieves.

Andrew H. Christian, January 1931. *Courtesy of Archer Christian Burke.*

I remember the watermelon, vegetable and ice wagons, drawn by mules, plodding slowly up the street with a young boy calling out his wares—"waa-ter-mel-on, but-ter beans, gr-een peas, ice"—and the gash I received between my eyes when I slipped on the icy sidewalk and hit the sharp corner of one of the stone steps leading to our house; the scar remains, as there were no plastic surgeons then. I remember the smell of corduroy by April 15. My brother, Andy Christian, Frank Stringfellow, Billy Preston and probably Billy Hill and I, the only eight-year-old girl, were in a carpool to St. Christopher's and St. Catherine's. The boys' corduroy knickers and knee-high wool socks were never changed from October to April (but they must have been cleaned, right?). You can imagine the aroma.

I remember the bootlegger who came to our house and siphoned spirits from a keg into my father's empty bottles through a long, narrow, pink rubber tube. The bottles were then locked in a closet until Thanksgiving, Christmas and other parties. I remember the sound of crickets and the feel of the burning sidewalk on my bare feet as we got out of the car on a hot August late afternoon after a carefree month at Virginia Beach. I remember peeling a tomato or peach and eating them like apples (they are not as good now) and the dank smell of oil, water, gasoline and dirt in every garage in town. I remember being pulled on sleds behind cars on a snowy winter afternoon; extreme caution was taken in case brakes were applied suddenly.

This carefree life ended with World War II. My father, Andrew Christian, who had served in World War I, left his law practice, joined the U.S. Air Force and served under General Chennault and his "Flying Tigers" in China. My brother joined the U.S. Marine Corps, was wounded twice (Saipan and Iwo Jima), won the Bronze Star and received a battlefield commission. My brother-in-law served as an officer in the U.S. Marine Corps and fought in several battles, including Guadalcanal.

When the men in our family returned from that conflict, they were all, especially my father, ardent admirers of Winston Churchill. It was therefore very exciting to learn that during Churchill's visit to Richmond soon after World War II, he would be driven down Monument Avenue right past our house, which faced the Lee monument. By then, we lived at number 1643. My father rushed into high gear, putting British and U.S. flags all over the front of our house and inviting everyone he saw to come to our porch to view the event. He could hardly contain himself until the moment finally arrived. "He's on his way"…"He's only three blocks away" were his news bulletins until we actually saw him coming. At the top of *our* performance (smiling, yelling and waving small flags), Churchill slowly turned his head to General Lee and gave him a long salute as if in slow motion. He never glanced our way, and the moment was over. Never have I seen such disappointment on all of our faces, but our admiration for the great man continues to this day.

As I close, I recollect that most of us were born in the neighborhood at Stuart Circle Hospital (named for J.E.B. Stuart, of course), which stood across from his monument. Most of us will end up as neighbors in Hollywood Cemetery, too, even if we lived elsewhere for years.

HOBSON GODDIN

E very neighborhood seemed to have at least one character living within its confines—someone living a rather different lifestyle than other neighbors. My Great-Uncle Saunders and Aunt Bessie Hobson seem to fit that pattern.

Sometime around 1935, they moved from their house in the 500 block of West Franklin Street to their new residence at 2324 Monument Avenue. The Hobsons had no children of their own, but the numerous neighbors' offspring immediately surrounded them. How did they survive? Years later, those children speak of the love and affection they had for them. Let me give you some background history.

Uncle Saunders, my great-uncle, was born on the family farm, Howard's Neck, in Goochland County shortly after "the war." The only resource left to the family was the land. Early on, at age fourteen, Uncle Saunders came to Richmond and was able to secure a job with Davenport & Company. He spent his days "scrubbing the Board" as the stock listings were recorded. He was a hard worker.

When he was about twenty-one years old, he was struck by lightning in the fields at Howard's Neck. Only a special train from Richmond, with a doctor aboard, saved him. But the fear of summer thunderstorms and lightning remained with him for the rest of his life. He would huddle in his house's English basement to escape any deadly bolts.

He continued his brokerage career with Davenport until his death in 1941, rising from the bottom to the top and becoming a millionaire in the depression years when millionaires were few and far between. He saved the family farm for his brothers and sisters, their families and their heirs. He had a rather gruff manner that hid his love of his neighbors and their children.

It has been said that lightning has a way of following something that it has victimized previously. A giant oak tree next to his section in Hollywood Cemetery was struck about seventy years ago, and now it bears its death wound.

Aunt Bessie was born in Albemarle County in a prominent family. Her playmates and friends included a wide circle; one in particular was Nancy Langhorne, later to become "Lady Astor," a member of the British Parliament. She visited Aunt Bessie frequently on Monument Avenue. When I visited Aunt Bessie, I was always on my "best manners," and I daresay that the neighbor's children, on their visits with her, likewise conformed.

It is pleasing to hear from the lips of the neighborhood children that they all remember Willis, Uncle Saunders' and Aunt Bessie's steadfast Mr. Everything, a man who kept an eye out for all of the neighborhood children, and to hear of the love and respect the neighborhood children held for Uncle Saunders and Aunt Bessie themselves. Their generosity was much appreciated in those dark days of the depression. At Christmastime, my brother, Alfred, and I would sit on the front steps at our home awaiting Willis in his job as chauffer to turn the corner in the car and deliver the small (in size) but much appreciated gift: a five-dollar gold piece. We both had spent the money several times over in our dreams for what we were going to buy. One year, Al misplaced his gold piece and could never find it. He always thought that he spent it in Mr. Brigg's Drug Store when he mistook it for a penny and bought three Mary Janes.

Nearby to our Monument Avenue houses, actually only two blocks away, stood the Broad Street Station, built in 1919 and serving the railways of that day (such as the Seaboard, the Atlantic Coast Lines and the Richmond, Fredericksburg and Potomac). In our younger days, we merely wished for a train ride, but as we grew older, our visions expanded as we watched the Orange Blossom Special and the Silver Meteor pull out of Broad Street Station en route to the warm, sunny beaches of Florida.

The station also served during World War II as brothers, relatives and friends departed for duty and service all over the world. Sadly, there were many in this group who failed to return.

Gone are the redcaps and taxis serving the many passengers, and gone, too, is the picture of General Eisenhower and Sir Winston Churchill emerging from the station and proudly riding down Monument Avenue to the capitol building.

A scene of another sort occurred in the station in the mid-1930s. A postal truck carrying valuable items was held up by Mais and Legenza (of the Tri-State Gang) on the overpass over the tracks. The driver was killed; the gangsters had

Back, left to right: Aunt Natalie Bocock and Dewey. *Front, left to right*: Miss Bessie Hobson (Mrs. Saunders Hobson) and Berta Bocock, holding Jack Bocock. Taken in the fall of 1964. *Courtesy of Roberta Bryan Bocock.*

also killed two policemen as they shot their way out of the penitentiary earlier. In due course, the gang was brought to justice, and Mais and Legenza were executed. Word got out that Legenza would be "laid out" for public inspection at the local funeral parlor in the 700 block of West Grace Street. Several of our neighborhood boys took it upon themselves to witness the event and stood in a long line for the viewing. Included in the group were Mason Williams and his little brother, Armistead. As we all waited on the sidewalk, along came Dr. and Mrs. Williams, driving home from St. Paul's Church. I still remember their horrified expressions as they snatched Mason and Armistead out of the line and drove away. Chastened, the rest of us took one quick peek, and then we, too, were gone!

We had a neighbor, whose name should be left unknown, who hated cats. As he sat on his porch, enjoying the breeze, the neighboring cats, of all breeds and sizes, would likewise gather on his porch, awaiting any handouts available. The old man grew more and more irate, as there were numerous strays throughout the area. One day, he stopped us boys and made a proposition. For every cat we killed, he would give us one dollar, with the cat to be shown to him and then dropped down the sewer. To us boys, that meant streetcar fare downtown, a candy bar and a movie. In due course, we did dispose of one cat and enjoy a western movie starring Tom Mix and a Babe Ruth candy bar. One of the boys started to talk about a cat having nine lives, so we recovered the dead cat from the sewer and displayed the dead cat to our patron, and he quickly forked over another dollar bill. To ease our trouble in recovering the cat, we tied a rope to his tail. About once a week, we would display the cat and receive our bounty. It was show time again. The cat did have about nine lives.

When the monument to General Lee was dedicated in 1891 on the proposed Monument Avenue, there were vast expanses of open countryside to the west. People questioned the placement of the monument so far out from the city. Even a tobacco field was close by the statue. Over the subsequent years, the city expanded, with new streets and avenues formed into blocks where new houses were built. What the city planners failed to foresee was the lack of open space for the residents, especially the children, with the exception of three triangles: one at Harrison Street, one at Lombardy Street and one at Meadow Street. These were quickly taken over by baby carriages and nannies. The median strip on Monument Avenue was too narrow for us to play serious ball, and the police chased us off there too.

So the young boys and girls were left to play ball on the sidewalks and streets. The depression helped to the extent that there were far fewer autos on the streets. West Avenue became our playground, with football, street hockey, roller skating and baseball, all in season. But the situation quickly worsened because of space restraints, and the activities moved to St. James's churchyard. Dr. Churchill Gibson was a local hero to kids for allowing children of all faiths to "play ball." Our families assumed the responsibility for paying for the broken windows, of which there were many.

The West Avenue All Stars played their games there with teams from Grace Street, Park Avenue and South Harrison Street. The games with Sauer's Garden and St. Christopher's were played on their more open lots. The sidewalks were all marked with white chalk for the girls' games of hopscotch and jumping rope. Old carriage steppingstones were perfect for Jack Rocks.

The lot next door to the Bemisses at the southwest corner of Allen Avenue and Monument was the scene of many hotly contested baseball games between the West Avenue boys and the Monument and Park Avenue boys.

LOUISE BRANDER
BUNNELL NEMECEK

Anyone who lived on Monument Avenue, especially from the early 1900s to the late 1950s, was privileged to be on such a beautiful street. The tree-lined grassplots, with the purple iris on each corner, the historic monuments, the large apartment buildings and the gracious homes, made it the most beautiful street in the city. From the Jeb Stuart monument at Stuart Circle to Stonewall Jackson's monument at the Boulevard, there were five churches, a school, a hospital, a dancing school and even a small castle. Some of the houses were so spacious that doctors had their offices in their residences.

Our family lived at 2012 Monument Avenue, a four-story home consisting of an entrance hall, a parlor, a living room, a dining room, a pantry and a kitchen. There were seven bedrooms, four bathrooms, two dressing rooms, two lavatories and a basement, but only five small closets. At one point, there were nine family members, made up of three generations, living in the house: my grandparents, William Mayo Taliaferro and Louise Brander; my parents, Frederick Hartsock Bunnell and Louise Taliaferro; my uncle, Thomas Brander Taliaferro; my great-uncle, Reverend William Walke Brander; my great-aunt, Elizabeth (Miss Lizzie) Walke Brander; my sister, Elizabeth Taliaferro Bunnell; me, Louise Brander Bunnell; and our little sister, Ellen Terry Bunnell.

Although she was not famous in the normal sense of the word, Miss Lizzie, as she was known to all, was reportedly considered quite a maverick for the time. She was the youngest of seven children, doted on by her five brothers and tolerated by her sister. She was a short and rather round little person who was considered a beauty in her day, with many suitors. She

(First two on left) the Laird twins, (third from left) Anne Lee Sanders Brown and Diana Hill (far right) with the Collegiate hockey team in front of Collegiate School. *Courtesy of William M. Hill.*

lamented the fact that she had not married because she could not find a man good enough for her. Much to my grandmother's chagrin, Miss Lizzie gambled at cards, played the ponies, smoked and thoroughly enjoyed her sherry. Needless to say, she was a "law unto herself" and kept all at number 2012 on their toes.

Many young children had nannies during our formative years, and our family was blessed with Lena Todd Carter. Our nannies pushed us up and down Monument Avenue in our baby buggies almost every day and would congregate at the triangle park at Meadow Street and Park Avenue, where we could play in the sandbox while the nannies socialized. Without my "Nennie,"

I would never have gone to school. It seems I was quite an incorrigible little person and threw tantrums unless Lena accompanied me to Collegiate every day. So Nennie and I graduated nursery school together. She was at the house in time to fix breakfast six days a week, took care of the three of us children, stayed to fix the family dinner and even joined the family each summer at the beach cottage. She not only helped to raise the three of us, but she also had thirteen children of her own. Talk about Wonder Woman! Lena was an interracial part of the fabric of our family. She was with us until stricken with cancer, and in her last days, my mother was at her bedside daily. I was seventeen when she died, and I vividly remember the minister's words at the funeral: "Lena is truly a saint gone to heaven." Lena was considered a member of the family, and it is impossible to express how much I loved my precious Nennie.

In those days, most people only had one family car. Walking, riding our bikes or strapping on our roller skates provided our transportation. As we got a bit older, we were allowed freedom that the children today can only dream of. We could leave the house in the morning and were only expected back by meal times. We played hopscotch on the sidewalks, tag on the grassplot and hide-and-seek in the yards and alleys. We could go to the Park Foodland and Reuben's deli at Meadow and Park or even venture to High's Ice Cream on Broad Street, and no one worried about us. In the summer, we would play under the lawn sprinklers to keep cool, and after a thunderstorm, we would wade in the gutters that were running with rainwater—delicious fun! We could walk to the movies, and when I was a bit older, I even rode my bike to and from the Country Club of Virginia to play tennis. The bikes of that day were sort of short and had fat tires. You really had to work hard to peddle them. They did not have gears, only brakes. Sometimes we peddled to Broad Street Station, where we would put a dime on the tracks and wait for the train to run over it. We would put the flattened coin on a chain to make a necklace—not *very* dangerous. Speaking of dangerous, we would climb the back fences and jump from one garage to another and considered it great fun.

Most everyone heated their houses with coal. It was delivered to our homes down a chute on the side of the house that went to a bin in the basement. In the winter, my father would go to the basement every night to take the burned clinkers out of the furnace and haul them out to the back gate. He had an old beat-up fedora that he called his "go to hell hat" because he said when he opened the furnace door, it was like facing the fiery flames of "down under." The heat was turned down at night, and I can vividly remember waking up in the morning to the distinct cracking sound of the hot water filling up the radiators throughout the house.

The coal was delivered from the alley behind Monument Avenue, as was the ice. We separated the garbage from the trash, not for recycling but to save the food scraps for the farmers. Certain cans were placed inside the back gate so the farmer could collect the garbage to feed his pigs. I'm sure the farmers were most appreciative, but the smell of the garbage drew very large rats to the alleys, a number of which were deposited on the front porch at number 2012 by Molly Bell Bunnell, Aunt Lizzie's cat.

Beside the furnace room in the basement was a large room with several stoves. Grandmother, Aunt Lizzie and Mother would put up watermelon pickles and green tomato pickles down there every summer. In the winter, they used the stoves to make plum puddings. The whole family would lend a hand in separating the raisins that came in clumps, picking the bread into small pieces and cutting up the suet. It was quite an operation, and the house was filled with wonderful, unforgettable aromas during those times.

As there were no washers or dryers, soiled clothing was placed in large woven baskets and taken to Annie Vanderval's house on Monday. Annie would wash and press all the clothes, fold them neatly and place them back into the basket for Friday pickup. Thank goodness there was a laundry that picked up the bed linens, curtains and such, or they would have had to be washed in the bathtubs.

Christmas Eve, we all went to church, where Daddy sang a solo of "O Holy Night." We went right to bed upon arriving home because Mother and Daddy had to make the eggnog and completely decorate the tree. I have always marveled as to how they managed to stay awake long enough to play Santa. Christmas night was always "open house" at number 2012, and my parents invited all their friends. There was a baby grand piano in the back hall, and there was a gentleman who came to play for the party. Everyone gathered around the piano and sang carols.

One of the things that made a large impression on me was what happened when people died. Large white wreaths were put on the doors to let everyone know that someone in that house had passed. At number 2012, our relatives' remains were brought to the house, and the caskets were placed in the parlor. Friends and neighbors would come to pay their respects and leave their calling cards. Chairs were brought in and placed in the entrance hall, living room and parlor, and the actual funeral services were held in the house. Our nanny would take all the children upstairs and try to keep us entertained, but we much preferred to watch the coming and goings from the third-floor windows.

During the war, we took in boarders. One of the gentlemen was Mr. Despary, an executive with Bethlehem Steel, and there were others as well. As a number of family members had passed away by that time, and Uncle

Brander was serving in the Philippines, there was room for the visitors on the third floor. Several soldiers from Fort Lee whom we had met at church would often come and stay on the weekends.

The children did their part for the war effort by jumping up and down on the empty tin cans to flatten them and by rolling tinfoil balls. Everyone purchased war bonds, and of course, we all used food stamps, as many foods were rationed. Daddy was an air raid warden. When the sirens would go off, he would don his hardhat and go out to patrol our block. Our job was to run all over the house to turn out the lights and close the curtains. This was a scary time, but we were not really old enough to understand what was happening, and most of our days were quite carefree.

Beside our house, there was an extra lot that ran the length of the house, with bushes, flowers and trees. It made a wonderful playground, and it was a great place for make-believe; one special tree was used for my Tarzan adventures. In the spring, my mother and godmother held a May Fair, and the yard was filled with tulips. People would come and order the bulbs from Holland for their gardens next year. When I was twelve, the side yard was used for what was called my "Baby Garden." There, in the summer of 1946,

Louise Brander Brunnell (Nemecek) in her mother's garden. *Courtesy of Louise Bunnell Nemecek.*

Everything stops for water and cookies at 10:30, and Louise sees that everybody's served and helps the little ones drink without spilling.

Louise Brunnell (Nemecek) holds nursery school. *Courtesy of Louise Bunnell Nemecek.*

I babysat for quite a number of children from the neighborhood. They would come to play for the morning. I charged six cents per hour and gave my little sister, Ellen Terry Bunnell, five cents per day to help at snack time and take the little ones to the bathroom. The *News Leader* did an article on the enterprise—it must have been desperate for news!

When sister Bet became a teenager, Mother and Daddy were chaperones almost every Friday and Saturday night for Betty's friends. The player piano sounded rolls in the hall, and the Victrola played records in the living room. The rugs were rolled up and everyone danced. I would sneak out of bed and sit on the backstairs to observe the festivities. To this day, Betty's friends tell me that they remember when they rolled up the rugs at number 2012 to dance.

One of my favorite memories is the Sunday afternoon walks to the Boulevard with my father, "Freddy B." These would often take several hours as we stopped to visit many Monument Avenue residents sitting out on their porches. We certainly lived in a kinder and gentler time growing up on our beautiful street. You knew most of your neighbors, and people were concerned about one another. The feeling of being safe in your surroundings was very apparent. I do not remember ever seeing a key to number 2012, and I do not believe we ever locked the front door. We were truly blessed to be raised on Monument during our childhood years.

ANNE WILLSON
HARRISON EASTMAN

Number 2023 Monument Avenue was my home from May 1929 to April 1942. During my childhood, the avenue was totally residential and peaceful, with very little turnover. Our house faced north, and so we had little or no sun on the font of the house, but whenever it snowed, the snow stayed on my side of the street for a long, long time. In 1940, there was an enormous snowstorm in Richmond that brought the city to a halt. The story goes that the mayor left for Florida. Richmond had only one plow and could barely cover anything, and so men walked to and from work as wheeled transportation could not move. We were able to play in the snow in front of my house for days and days.

One of the greatest treasures, to my mind, of living on Monument Avenue during the 1920s, '30s and '40s was the experience of being with those wonderful ladies who were nurses to the children of that time. The ones I remember most clearly were Clara with the Wellfords, Lelia with the Christians, Lena with the Bunnells, Martha with the Augustines (technically they lived on Park Avenue, but she and Lucy Carter played with us every afternoon) and, most of all, Hattie Royall with me (the Harrisons). All the children as well as the parents called her Nanna. She explained that Nanna means nurse.

In good weather, nurses and children would gather on the sunny (south) side of Monument, often in front of Billy Hill's house since the sidewalk seemed wider there. The nurses would hold the rope ends for jump rope or watch us floundering on roller skates. In the spring, we often met on

Ann Willson Harrison in the arms of her nurse, Hattie Royall. *Courtesy of Ann Willson Harrison Eastman.*

the grassplots, where we collected new dandelion growth for them to make dandelion wine for their respective churches.

Nanna (and I imagine it may have been true of the others) taught me to ride my bicycle, knit and sew on a button, as well as anything useful/ practical that I have ever learned. She had two rules to live by that she passed along. One was that "you got to have patience," and the other, said over and over, was that "manners will get you farther than money." Nanna and these other women exemplified boundless patience, dignity and love beyond measure to their charges.

My best friend, Betty Bunnell, lived across the street at 2012 Monument Avenue. When I was old enough to cross alone, we played in her yard for sun and warmth in the winter and then at my house when summer came and we wanted to stay cool in the shade. The signal to each of us when it was time to go home was seeing the automobile lights. When they showed up, each of us went to her own house. We learned to roller skate as well as ride bicycles on Monument Avenue. Being able to do both up and down the block with no oversight gave us an unparalleled sense of freedom.

Either there was no street crime or our families were terrifyingly naïve since no one worried about our being on the sidewalk alone, crossing the street at dusk or even visiting a neighbor's house without telling anyone. I knew the people who lived in each house on my side of the street and in my block, and I would go visit from time to time just to say hello. It seemed a perfectly normal thing to do. At about age nine or ten, Betty and I would go around the corner to Reuben's to buy half-pint containers of orange sherbet. We would come back to her house and sit on her front steps to eat this treat and watch the cars go by. It was pure heaven.

One of my lasting memories of that beautiful, wide and tree-lined street was watching a "show of force" parade by the Virginia State Guard near the beginning of the Second World War. I was playing at Betty's, and a rumor started that there was to be a riot in the city on Memorial Day. So, the State Guard (of which my father was a member) assembled and paraded down Monument Avenue, ostensibly to honor Memorial Day but actually to send a message to the numerous potential rioters (who never showed up). Last came a group representing the Daughters of the Confederacy. These women were dressed head to toe in unrelieved black, flowing veils and all. They looked to us like an escaped group from some witches' coven. Each woman carried a wreath that they planned to put in Hollywood Cemetery at the Confederate soldiers' monument. To this day, I can still see those veils blowing in the wind and the determined looks on the faces of those women. Betty and I were struck dumb with awe.

The medians with irises, 1924. *Courtesy of the Valentine Richmond History Center.*

In later years, when I visited, I remember my first "Monument Avenue Day," when the street was blocked off and everyone with a dog brought it out for a walk about. What a glorious time to see all those great animals. I also remember being so surprised at how the occupancy of the street had changed from family homes to student houses from the college; its name, too, changed so many times—from a William and Mary extension to RPI, VCU and probably one or two in between—that I don't remember what it was called at the time. Most of the student-occupied houses had some sort of floral flag hanging out front. Sadly, the Iris "flags" at the ends of the grassplots are gone.

Monument Avenue was and is a beautiful street. Wonderful houses, with no two alike, are a joy to see to this day. I hope Monument will continue to age with grace, dignity and beauty.

JOHN HOWE CECIL JR.

In 1925, my parents moved to 2314 Monument Avenue, just east of President Jefferson Davis's monument. This is the block where the Confederate cannon that marks the outer line of Richmond's defenses during the Civil War sits in the middle of the grassplot in front of our house. This cannon, remarkably, points directly at President Davis's monument. In fact, when I am asked about my memories of spending the first fifteen years of my life on the beautiful part of Monument Avenue, the first thing I recall today is the amazing and, in my opinion, somewhat odd collection of monuments: the tallest for the president of the Confederacy, then three heroic Confederate generals on horseback, a famous naval explorer, an international champion tennis player (who was a Richmond native) and a cannon from the War Between the States.

A few years after I was born, two sisters, Patricia Cary Cecil and Jane Coejman Abert Cecil, joined our family. Others in our household in the 1930s included an aunt, Miss Sallie Campbell Cary, and my first cousin, Miles Fairfax Cary, better known as "Fax." Fax came to live with us in 1934 after both of his parents had died, and my father adopted him. He was three years older than I was and had a very friendly, outgoing and adventurous personality. When he moved in, a number of his old friends from his former neighborhood near the Robert E. Lee monument joined us for touch football and other healthy activities on the Monument Avenue grassplot.

These other activities included neighborhood boys climbing on President Davis's very tall monument. One unusual feature of this memorial was that

The cannon, on the 2300 block grassplot, marks the line of Richmond's outer defenses during the Civil War. It is aiming directly at President Jefferson Davis. *Courtesy of the Valentine Richmond History Center.*

it was surrounded by a fence topped with steel spikes pointing straight up. Being conservative types who occasionally thought about living to a ripe old age, some of us did hesitate before trying to climb all the way to the top.

A noteworthy event for "progressive" Monument Avenue residents occurred when I was two or three years old. At that time in the 1920s, there

John Cecil and his sister, Pat, on the front porch of number 2314 in the summer of 1932. *Courtesy of Patricia Cary Cecil Hass.*

was a child-rearing theory, I have been told, that children of both sexes would play best when they were not clothed. The educational theory became very popular for a few years. So, my mother and a group of her friends used to gather many of my contemporaries with me in the summer—a whole gaggle of children—in our backyard. The yard had a lovely ivy-covered brick wall around it so we couldn't escape and people couldn't see us all running around naked. That is, the general public couldn't see us, but Mrs. Robert Bryan lived next door at number 2312, with back windows overlooking our yard. Considering proper peoples' opinions on public nakedness at that time, I suspect that she got the surprise of her life. I don't know that she said anything to our mother, but our maternal grandmother, Mrs. T. Archibald Cary, lived on the other side of us, and since she was a very religious lady, I have been told she was not a supporter of the project. I have also been told that my younger sister, Pat, participated with her contemporaries a few years later, but I was not allowed to attend those events. Whatever the fallout, we all had a wonderful time, and as far as I recall, this experience did not produce traumas in any of us.

Some of those child-rearing theories were probably also endorsed by the teachers at the first school we attended, now known as Albert H. Hill, which used to be known as Richmond Normal School, a teacher training institution. Miss Bailey and Miss Nesbitt, who were famous throughout the community, were the leaders of that "progressive" school. It had an excellent reputation, and we all loved it. As it was only an elementary school, many of us left after the fifth grade and went our separate ways to St. Christopher's or St. Catherine's, but the influence of those two ladies stayed with us for the rest of our lives.

In 1937, I believe, there was an outstanding episode on our block that received both police and newspaper attention. On Halloween evening, Fax and I, along with another "Civil War veteran" who was visiting from Park Avenue, formed a "plan of action." We collected some firecrackers that we had saved from the Fourth of July and secretly removed the black powder and fuses from them (without my parents' knowledge, of course). Then, we took the powder and fuses, added a small collection of old newspapers and an old rusty chain and quietly approached the cannon in the middle of the grassplot.

At that time, the cannon's barrel was completely open, and there was also a hole in the top into which Confederate cannoneers poured powder and stuck the fuses. So we stuffed newspapers in the barrel, packed them in tight and pushed the chain in front. Then, of course, being knowledgeable cannoneers, we poured our black powder down the hole in the top of the cannon, followed by our longest fuse. Though this was a lot of work, we did it all in complete silence, keeping a lookout for passing cars or other enemies. Since this was 1937, there was nothing like the traffic there is today. Very few cars passed by. When a car did come, we would hide behind the cannon base so its headlights wouldn't pick us up. Even if they did, the driver would think we were just boys out visiting neighbors on Halloween night.

I don't know who lit the match. I was too young to smoke at that time, but someone—and I won't say who—had a match, lit it and touched it to the fuse. The cannon went off with a tremendous boom, rattling all the windows in the neighborhood and shooting the chain straight up the middle of the grassplot. Fortunately, as the cannon barrel was horizontal, the missile trajectory was also horizontal, so it didn't endanger President Davis at all. But people rushed out of their houses, including my father. Of course, the principal mystery of this shocking and startling episode was the immediate and complete disappearance of the cannoneers. City officials were clueless. Their only recourse was to plug the barrel of the cannon with cement.

Although Fax went off to boarding school the next fall, and I was sent off two years later, we kept our military secret until we were no longer in Richmond, subject to a terrible punishment for so wicked a deed. Besides, I always felt that, as Fax and our cohort were three years older than I, that age difference meant that I should be deemed a juvenile, guiltless of anything that had occurred. But this episode explains why many experts have claimed that the cannon on our Monument Avenue block fired the very last shot of the War Between the States and, indeed, celebrated the final end of that conflagration. (Reenactors' cannons don't count.)

PATRICIA CARY CECIL HASS

I grew up at 2314 Monument Avenue with my brother, John, and my sister, Jane. There were a number of children on our block or living nearby, and we were looked after not only by parents and nurses but also by every household's butlers, cooks and maids. They all knew us, and we all knew them, and although woe did bestride us if we did anything truly bad, we felt very safe in that extraordinarily privileged and carefree environment.

At that time, there were no children's soccer, lacrosse or hockey weekends involving hapless parents carpooling children to endless games. On the weekends, our fathers went to the Commonwealth Club on Saturday or to the country club, where they played golf. *Our* weekends were wonderfully our own, and we used our imaginations to entertain ourselves. I don't remember ever being bored; on the contrary, we were always full of ideas for things to do. We rode our bikes, roller skated and ran all over in a world of freedom and beauty that is hard to imagine today. We rode our bikes to the Broad Street Station to buy comic books at its big newsstand, and we made ourselves capes, masks and even tights, though those soon got discarded as being too hot, and played Batman and Robin all over the block.

We discovered Little Orphan Annie and Dick Tracy from the Big Little books we got for Christmas and our birthdays. These were essentially comics enclosed in small, square, hardcover books that everyone cherished and refused to trade. Of course, some of the things we did were a bit unfortunate. I remember one episode when my cousin Russell Cecil's parents brought him and his governess to visit us. Maybe because our fathers were brothers,

Russell and I were soul mates from birth, close to the same age and set each other off like electrical sparks. We were full of mischievous ideas at every turn. So when Russell came to Richmond, I felt I had to show him all that Monument Avenue had to offer. The thrill of a few trips to the bowling alley soon wore off, so one day, when our nurses brought our lunch trays out on the side porch, Russell felt inspired to point out Mrs. Bryan's lovely gothic windows, which faced the porch. Grinning, he dared me to hit one with my mashed potatoes. At this time, we were about six years old, and I had been *dared*. I stood up, grabbed a handful of mashed potatoes and threw, *hard*. I hit a window! What a satisfying *splat*. I threw again and heard another *splat*. Now I was joined by my giggling cousin, throwing his peas, throwing his tomatoes, throwing his entire lunch. It all hit Mrs. Bryan's windows. I followed suit, and then we ran.

Screeching nurses' voices followed us as we tore along the side of the house into the back garden, where we dove under a huge forsythia bush, refusing to come out. It was extremely thick and very prickly, so the nurses were not able to grab us, and by the time my parents and Russell's parents were summoned, we began to wail—mostly from terror, definitely not from remorse. Mercifully, I have no recollection of what happened after that. What did my mother say to Mrs. Bryan? What *could* she say? In those days of rigid behavior, how was my mother going to explain our actions without being permanently disgraced as to the way she was raising her children? I will never know, but I have never forgotten how much fun that lunch it was for Russell and for me.

That back garden at number 2314 was one of our best playgrounds. Aside from the big forsythia bush along the brick wall and the dogwood trees in a corner of that same wall, where we could hide, we climbed the fig tree and picked figs (sometimes falling out); my brother and his friends built a circular track and raced their bikes; we had animal pens and swing sets; we had dog hurdles; and we had a pigeon coop; we built a waterfall on the bank by the terrace and then dug a pit under it to make a lake for our toy boats. Mr. Gillette had designed the garden for our mother, but she let us do all those things out there, frequently ruining the grass. She just said she was raising children, not grass, and that was that. I never knew what Mr. Gillette thought.

On Sunday, everyone went to church, with very few exceptions. Our family went to Second Presbyterian, but there were also St. James's and St. Paul's, where most of the Monument Avenue families we knew went. Sunday school was de rigueur for the children, and there we were taught the gospel of charity. We were made to understand that there were many people

Pat Cecil and her mother in front of number 2314, February 1932. *Courtesy of Patricia Cecil Hass.*

with far fewer worldly goods than our own, particularly as America was then in the throes of the Great Depression. Even our schools instilled in us that it was more blessed to give than to receive. I remember going almost weekly with older relatives to other parts of the city with clothes and baskets of food, especially big at Thanksgiving, Christmas and Easter. We children tried to invent moneymaking schemes to buy toys for those baskets, most of which never panned out. We tried setting up our circus toys on the sidewalk and doing a show, hoping that people would drop money in the paper cups we were thrusting at them. But as the 2300 block was a very proper block and our mother wouldn't let us put up a sign, the passersby, with sickly smiles, just stumbled over the toys and kept going.

But when our aunt (who lived next door at number 2320 with our grandmother, Mrs. T. Archibald Cary) moved in with us at number 2314 after our grandmother died, we found a much more suitable way to raise money, even if it was for mistreated animals instead of hungry people. Aunt Cammie was president of the Richmond SPCA, and she imbued us with sympathy for stray and mistreated animals. We all had pets—the usual dogs and cats plus various other animals like canaries, rabbits, baby chickens, pigeons; you name it and we had it, except for cows and horses. Some of us even had those, up in the country on our families' farms. So we decided to do something to help that worthy institution, and putting on a pet show was a natural.

All the children on our block participated, as well as others from blocks down the avenue and on Park. For days before the show, we planned our acts, trained our animals and wrote out tickets. In spite of our earlier depredations, our butler, William, was able to get the garden presentable, and on the chosen day, wild with excitement, we watched as our mother supervised the preparations. Chairs were put on the terrace, iced tea and little sandwiches were readied and at 4:00 p.m. the audience, the grande dames of the block, arrived. Mrs. John Kerr Branch, Mrs. Saunders Hobson, the two Mrs. Bryans, Mrs. Gordon Wallace (from Park Avenue) with Mrs. John Lea, Mrs. Coleman Wortham, Cousin Lily Wilson and so on. Instead of paying the ten-cent admission, these ladies gave us more. Some gave one dollar, a few gave five dollars and, joy of joys, Mrs. Branch gave us ten dollars!

They sat on our terrace and watched as we went through our acts, applauding each time. Flushed with pleasure, after the grownups had eaten the sandwiches and drunk the iced tea, we were rewarded with Dr. Peppers and cookies. Then, we put the ticket money in a big jar and crowded into Aunt Cammie's car. She drove us straight to the SPCA, where, proudly and with a huge sense of a job well done, we made our donation, the first of what became an annual occurrence. (This is probably why, when my sister, Jane, grew up, she eventually became a board member and then president of the Richmond SPCA.)

This was not the only event our mother hosted. I remember many parties—teas, receptions, Christmas parties, debutante parties and formal dinners; they seemed part of our lives. Our Cecil and Cary families were large in number, and although most lived in Richmond or elsewhere in the state, others had moved to New York or Long Island, and they all loved to come back to Richmond to visit. Because our mother was so welcoming, they usually stayed at our house, which was large and could easily accommodate guests. When my older cousins "came out" as debutantes, many admirers arrived in Richmond in hot pursuit. These gentlemen were also housed with us, as was deemed proper, rather than in the debutantes' own houses.

One of these beaux was the British film star David Niven. He had met our beauteous cousin Elizabeth Cecil Cary in Bermuda when she was vacationing there with relatives, and he was en route to Hollywood to start what became an auspicious movie career. Completely smitten, he followed her to Richmond, where my Aunt Elizabeth Cecil Scott, unimpressed, sent him to our house, where he was lodged in a bedroom suite on the third floor. I remember coming out of my room one morning and seeing this nice-looking man bounding down the third-floor stairs. We met in the second-floor hall, and he said good morning, but as I had been taken to see *Alexander's Ragtime Band* and had fallen madly in love with the gorgeous Tyrone Power, I was indifferent. I was also hungry for breakfast, so I only said a hurried good morning back. However, he sat next to me at breakfast and made an effort to be friendly, so I decided he was nice and told this to my Cousin Betty. Unfortunately, she didn't feel the same way, and after a week of his tooling her around Richmond in a borrowed convertible, she told him so. Well mannered to the end, he said goodbye.

Things slowed down when World War II descended on the world, and everyone began pitching in for the "war effort." In school, we were instructed to save paper by writing on the back as well as the front of our notebook pages. We were encouraged to knit squares for blankets for European refugees and were allowed to knit in our classes if our grades were A- or above or in study hall if we had finished our homework. We could even knit in Assembly. The teachers collected the squares, and the older girls spread them out on lunch tables and sewed them together into blankets. Since our yarns could be any color we liked, I remember how colorful our blankets were, and I remember wishing I could meet some of the people who got them, particularly the children, and hoping our blankets had helped to keep them warm. We didn't know about the death camps then, but we did know there were many refugees elsewhere, including British children who'd been shipped out of London to escape the Blitz and sent to America to spend "the duration" in our cities with hospitable families. I remember thinking how horrible it would be to be one of those children, having to leave their fathers and mothers and travel three thousand miles on a ship to stay safe.

The practice air raids began right away, so in the daytime, no matter where you were, you had to take cover. Often I was somewhere on my bike when the siren sounded, and I knew I had to get off, go up to the nearest house and ring the doorbell. They had to take you in, no matter what. It says a lot about the times we grew up in that no one gave a thought that this might be dangerous for a young girl—our country was different then and far safer. Americans were a different kind of people too. What I remember most is that almost everyone was truly behind the war, and unlike today, people were very patriotic. Very few people cheated on their ration books for gas, sugar, meat and butter or whatever else was in short supply. Today, our population seems far more dishonest, but then people looked down on the cheaters and tried their best to do without and not complain. After all, everyone knew families who'd lost someone in the fighting—certainly almost every family had someone serving overseas (in our family's case, it was five young men)—and it would have been unforgivable for us at home not to back them up. Families also opened their homes to the servicemen stationed at the camps around Richmond, many of whom went to our churches and got invited for Sunday dinner. They got the best food, too.

Of course, there was gas rationing—three gallons per week per car. We were lucky because we had two cars, but even so, the gas wasn't used to drive children anywhere unless it was raining hard or you were sick. We saved our gas for rare vacation trips to the beach or to the mountains. I rode my bike the five blocks to my school, Collegiate, and my sister took the streetcar to St. Catherine's in Westhampton. Servants came to work on the streetcars too. Our mother used the car to go to church or to shop at Miller & Rhoads and Thalhimers, the two big department stores downtown where everyone shopped in those days. For deliveries, some stores dragged out old wagons and used horses, or boys put huge baskets on their bikes, making them look so top-heavy you wondered if they could stay upright.

Meat, sugar, eggs and butter were all scarce, although we had margarine, which was white and looked disgustingly like lard. It came in packages with a yellow capsule you broke over it in a bowl and squished around enough to make it yellow. Tin cans were recycled—aluminum was an essential part of airplanes—and we rode our bikes to a collection spot on Broad Street. We got used to being freezing cold in the winter, as fuel oil for our big houses' furnaces was in very short supply. The heat could be turned on in the morning for two hours and another two again in the evening, but the rest of the time we were cold, cold, cold, although we did have fireplaces and used them when we could get wood. Coal was in short supply as well since the miners had gone off to war.

The summers were equally hard because with not enough gas to drive anywhere to cool off and with heavy blackout curtains in the living room and dining room and front hall closed, there was no way to escape the heat, as no one had air conditioning of course. Luckily, in the summer, the country was on something called "double daylight" time, so it was still light while we ate dinner, and the servants could see to clean up in the kitchen and get home before dark. After that, people would sit out on their side porches in the pitch dark to cool off. But it was not very cool.

Finally, the war ended, and once again our mother took up her hostess duties, as people began to travel again. Our English cousins, the Sitwells of literary fame, were among the first to come to America. They loved visiting Richmond and dining at our mother's table. They came quite often, in fact, though never all together. I don't remember much about Dame Edith except that my Aunt Cammie was heard to say she was "difficult," but I became quite fond of Sir Osbert and his younger brother, Sacheverell. When I was old enough to drive, I took Osbert to Williamsburg once or twice and Sacheverell to his favorites, the James River plantations. All in one day was too much for my mother, which was one of the reasons I was chosen. I think the English gentlemen were unused to teenage female chauffeurs, but once they realized I loved books and could actually converse (what young southern lady could not?), they relaxed and we got on famously. Some years later, we visited them in England at their family estate, Renishaw, and found that they remained as funny, savvy and brilliant as ever.

Looking back, my childhood on Monument Avenue sometimes seems like a lovely dream, quick to dissolve in the light of day. But on a glorious June afternoon, it's easy to picture it all again—the birds serenading us from those same branches and the sun shining into our windows through a cloud of puffy green maple trees. Or I see a winter day, with the branches of those same trees stark and black against a rose and lavender sunset behind the Jefferson Davis monument. I can see snow falling gently or the purple irises at the ends of the grassplot in the spring. I can see us as children, running all around, riding our bikes and shrieking with joy that we have finally learned how to stay upright. In those moments, my childhood returns and makes me smile, and then I know that Monument Avenue will stay in my heart forever.

JANE ABERT CECIL

Growing up in our house at number 2314 had many wonderful advantages. We lived on a beautiful avenue, of course, but what was generally less recognized was the very convenient location as well. Within three or four blocks we had the Capitol movie theater, First and Merchants Bank, Broad Street Station and High's Ice Cream Store. At the corner of Broad and Meadow Streets was Mr. Hawthorne's Drug Store, located in a long, triangular-shaped building. In addition, a lady named Miss Fry held her tap and ballet dancing classes for children a block and a half from us on Robinson Street. Her studio was in the basement of an apartment building, but it had above-ground windows, so if you walked by on the way to the bank or to Broad Street, you could hear not only the lively music but also the sound of tapping feet.

When I was little, I had a Nannie, and every afternoon we would go out to one or more of these places. I didn't go to the movies then, but we would look at the pictures outside and see what was playing at the Capitol. When we went by Miss Fry's windows, I always tried to look down inside because my sister, Pat, took lessons there. Lots of her friends did too, and later I knew it was because lots of mothers wanted their little girls to be like Shirley Temple, right down to the corkscrew curls. But Nannie usually pulled me along to keep going.

I especially liked going to Mr. Hawthorne's. We would sit on the stools at the counter and have lemonade. If we didn't do that, we would get an ice cream cone at High's or walk to Broad Street Station to watch the trains

Robinson Street, with its streetcar tracks crossing Monument Avenue. Miss Fry's Dance Studio is on the left. *Courtesy of the Valentine Richmond History Center.*

as they pulled into or left Richmond. Sometimes we would go to the Old Soldier's Home on the Boulevard. This required a ride in the stroller, coming or going. Nannie liked to talk to the old soldiers, and I liked to look at the real stuffed horse in the middle of the hall. He belonged to a general in the war. I never knew why the general stuffed his horse and left him there. It was even more confusing when the general and his horse were pointed out to me on the top of a monument. Later, I found out that that horse was named Little Sorrel, and he belonged to General Stonewall Jackson.

When I was five, Nannie took me to First and Merchants Bank to open a savings account. The teller gave me a bankbook with three dollars stamped on the front page. This was very exciting, and I kept the book under my pillow for a long time.

Sometimes Daddy would come home from work, park in front of the house and collect Mother, Pat and me to go for a ride in the country. In those days, we didn't have to go far to be in the country. We usually went out Staples Mill Road to Glen Allen to put pennies on the railroad track. The

The equestriennes, Jane and Pat Cecil, 1937. *Courtesy of Patricia Cecil Hass.*

5:30 p.m. train would come along and smash them flat. The engineer always waved and blew the whistle.

The whole family was very fortunate to have our "live-in" Aunt Cammie, whom we called Com. Most Saturdays, she would take Pat and me to the Children's Department at Richmond's main Public Library, which was downtown on Franklin Street. We each could get six books. Pat read much faster than I did, so she usually helped me select my books until Com would say, "No Pat, let Jane pick her own."

Com would also take us to the Brook Run Stables off Staples Mill Road, where we learned to ride. I learned to get on and off a horse, walk and trot. Fortunately for me, Com would always ride with us, and we usually went over to Monument Avenue because it wasn't paved and there was almost no traffic. Pat liked to canter and would race up to Horsepen Road and back, but I wasn't enthusiastic about going so fast nor did I like to cross Broad Street, where there was enough traffic to make me and the horse uneasy. I usually got off the horse and walked him across. Pat and Com never did that.

During the 1930s and early '40s, I remember the "hobos" (our mother called them poor, jobless men) who would ring the doorbell and ask for money or food. Mother never gave them money because she was afraid they would use it for beer, but she always gave them a sandwich, chips, cookies, water and juice. I was not supposed to watch them eat, but when they rang the bell again, I could answer the door and take the glasses and plates back. They always said thank you, and I know we had repeat visitors. I kept wondering who they were and what had happened to make them so poor.

I think one way the Great Depression filtered into our consciousness was seeing those men and hearing the adults talk about the poverty. They didn't think we heard, but we did, and I think it accounted for the older children inventing schemes for making money. One of their schemes got me into trouble. When I was five or six, my sister, Pat, and I had some very good friends, Betty Bowe and Grace Wallace. One day, Pat and Betty Bowe were making artificial flowers in front of our house and selling little bunches for a nickel to passersby. In those days, people walked a lot, and they often walked the avenue. It looked like fun, and I wanted to help, but Betty and Pat wouldn't let me stand there with them, announcing that I was too young. I think they wanted all the money for themselves.

When they'd sold out and gone inside, I went over to the house next door, Mrs. Bryan's, at number 2312. She had gorgeous azaleas in the front yard, and as it was springtime, they were all in bloom. I collected a few, tied strings around them and added bows. I thought they were prettier than the artificial ones Pat and Betty Bowe had made, but I didn't have as much luck as they'd had, so I gave up, went in and showed my mother what was left. She was absolutely horrified. She told me to go right back over to see Mrs. Bryan and tell her what I'd done and how sorry I was. I was mortified because I had thought it was such a smart idea, but I knew I had to go. I don't know whether Mother called Mrs. Bryan or not, but I went over there scared to death. The chauffeur, James, answered the door when I rang. I said, "Mother says I have to talk to Mrs. Bryan and tell her I'm sorry." I hoped maybe James would tell Mrs. Bryan for me, but no, he said that she was waiting for me in the library. So I followed him back to where she was sitting, looking very serious. Quivering, I said, "Mrs. Bryan, I am really sorry, but they were so pretty, and Pat and Betty Bowe wouldn't let me sell the artificial ones with them. I thought maybe you'd wouldn't mind, but Mother says it was really bad, and I'm sorry."

Mrs. Bryan didn't smile. She told me not to do it again, and I left, feeling very ashamed. When I remember that episode, I still do.

When I was little, the whole family went to Florida right after Christmas. My father had business to do in Miami Beach and would travel back and forth to Richmond and New York. Every winter, we stayed several months and enjoyed the sea, sand and warm weather. John and Pat went to school while we were there. Most of the family drove down in two days and in two cars, but Nannie and Pat and I took the "sleeper" down and back. I thought that was the name of the train, but Nannie said it meant that everybody who got on the train had to go to sleep.

I remember one particular trip very well. I had been put to bed at my usual bedtime and then awakened and dressed in a coat, hat, mittens and a blanket. Cousins Lucius and Virginia Cary arrived to take me, Nannie and Pat to the train, which was waiting for us at Broad Street Station. It was dark and cold, and the train was very big, making a noise and blowing smoke. I was clutching my doll, and as we were saying goodbye and starting to board, I realized that my doll's trunk was missing. We had left it behind, and I wouldn't go without it. I don't remember exactly what happened next, but I do remember that Cousin Lucius said that he would rush back to our house and get the trunk from the front hall. I thought we had a very nice conductor who said he would hold the train for a few minutes. Since there were no traffic lights and few cars at 10:30 p.m., Cousin Lucius made it to Monument Avenue and back in record time. I went happily to sleep in the Pullman berth with my doll, and for many years, "Uncle Lucius" was my favorite cousin.

Daddy would take the night train to and from New York once or twice a week. Years later, when I rode the train to college and gave the ticket seller my name, he asked me if I was related to Mr. John Cecil. It seems that Daddy was very popular at the station. That may have been why the conductor was willing to hold our Florida train for a few minutes, but the engineer probably knew that he could make up the time. When we arrived in Miami, Daddy and Mother were there to meet us.

Coming home in the spring, the train would leave Miami in the afternoon, and there was always a small band on the rear deck of the caboose playing "Moon Over Miami." We always felt sad to be leaving but happy to get back home to Monument Avenue, where spring was usually in full bloom.

Our Florida winter trips ended with the advent of World War II, because civilian railway travel was discouraged—the army needed the tracks to transport troops and weapons—and there was not the gasoline to drive. But at that time, jobs became more plentiful, due to defense work, and the impoverished men stopped coming. But now we had practice air raids during the day, which was not so bad. At night, though, a lot more was involved. The hideously loud sirens would sound off, and if it was nighttime, Pat and I would run around the house closing the windows and pulling down the black shades. We had some kind of tape that we would use to seal the floppy shades to the window frames. Then we would find a place in the middle of the floor and read very carefully by flashlight. The adults in the house would just sit and wait until the all-clear sounded, and we would turn the lights back on.

Our mother had been asked to be a spotter for enemy planes. She would go to Broad Street Station (now the Science Museum) once or twice a month and stay about four hours, usually in the evenings. I remember asking her how she would identify the enemy. She said there were usually five or six other people there, and they had big picture of German planes and special binoculars. It would have been exciting if she had seen an enemy plane, but she never did. For quite some time, the air raids would happen once a month, but their frequency eventually decreased.

In the spring, my mother and many of our neighbors were accustomed to having the winter rugs cleaned, stored and replaced by lightweight or straw summer rugs. This work was always done by Mr. Yonan, who also had beautiful Oriental and Middle Eastern rugs for sale. He would come to our house in late May with two or three helpers to collect our rugs and put down the straw ones. I would be waiting at the door to let them in, and he would always ask mother if I could ride with him to help at the other houses. This was a ritual. Mother would protest that I would be in the way, but we all knew that she would let me go. It was such fun! I sat on the rugs in the front of his truck—sometimes so high that I couldn't see out of the window. At each house, he would take me in, introduce me to the owner as Mrs. Cecil's youngest daughter and say something about my being thirsty. I would usually be rushed off to the kitchen by the maid or cook for milk and cookies. He would bring me home in time for lunch too full to eat but hoping to tell about my trip to anyone who would listen. Mother always asked me if I had thanked everyone, especially Mr. Yonan. This entertainment would be reversed in the fall. If school were in session, he would come on a Saturday. I did this until I was ten or eleven, and I still remember loving it. Mr. Yonan was a very special person.

One hot summer day when I was about twelve, I went up to the third floor of our house to poke around the attic. Sometimes Pat and I would find something to do or wear or find cabinets to go through. But Pat wasn't with me that day, and I didn't have the energy nor her imagination to make something out of the many boxes. I did think about trying on some old Confederate or World War I uniforms and marching downstairs, but they were dusty, heavy and hot and smelled funny. Instead, I opened the one dormer window, thinking that even warm fresh air would improve the stifling attic. Then I remembered that we had been out that window before and onto the flat tin roof to look down at our backyard. So up and out I went. I walked carefully to the edge of the roof and saw all the backyards. No one was outside. It was too hot.

It occurred to me that we had never gone to the top of the sloping green tiled roof, which covered the main part of the house. That was an interesting challenge that I was sure I could manage. I would use the dormer window to boost myself up, and if I slipped, I would end right back on the flat roof and not on the sidewalk. So up I went. It wasn't as easy as it looked, but my tennis shoes were a big help. When I got to the top, I straddled the roof, which was warmer than I thought it would be, but my jeans made it bearable. The view was incredible. I saw rows and rows of maple trees with bright green leaves, the top of the Jefferson Davis monument and many different types of roofs. I only looked to the west. As courageous as I thought I was, I decided that turning around might be a problem. Instead, I slid down the tiles to the flat roof, crawled into the attic and closed and locked the window. I wanted to tell Mother or someone about my adventure, but I thought better of it.

I climbed to the roof one more time that summer so that I could face east, but because I finally told Mother what I had done, she was not happy and that took the fun out of it. She told me never to do it again as it was too dangerous. However, in the fall, the beautiful colors of the maple leaves made me reconsider, so I asked her if I could go up one last time. Pat went out on the flat roof to stand below me, and William, our butler, sat in the attic window. I don't know what they would have done if I had fallen, but their presence relieved Mother's anxiety.

From the top, when I got there, it was a beautiful sight: Monument Avenue spread out below me in all its autumn finery. Now, whenever I think back to my childhood, that is one of my most vivid memories—the beautiful avenue where I grew up—and an integral part of me to this day.

GERTRUDE SKELTON BRYAN

My friends and family call me Trudy, and I grew up with my younger sister, Roberta Hamilton Bryan, called Berta, at 2326 Monument Avenue, just three doors west of Pat and Jane Cecil's house. Our mother and father, Gertrude Skelton Hobson and Alexander Hamilton Bryan, bought 2326 Monument from Dr. and Mrs. Robert Preston, who then moved out to a larger house, Fairfield, off River Road. Of course, we all knew one another, even though their children—Alice, Billy and Bobby—were older than we.

Aunt Sallie and Aunt Fannie, two maiden sisters out of ten living siblings of our grandfather, Alexis Corydon Hobson, told us when we were young girls about pulling Robert E. Lee's statue to its site on Monument Avenue by use of a cart and ropes. They expounded on the roar of excitement as the statue passed through the streets and was erected. They were able to get a hunk of the rope as a memento, but it has long since been lost.

Mrs. Saunders Hobson's house was next door to ours, at number 2324. As others have said, she was one of the great ladies of Richmond. I only vaguely remember Mr. Hobson, but I remember hearing many stories about him. For instance, he had his shirts laundered in New York, and someone from Davenport & Company would take the shirts up there on the train and go back a few days later to pick them up. He was also rumored to be a conductor of electricity, having been struck by lightning when he was a young man. Later, after he married Miss Bessie and they were living at number 2324, he was standing at their second-floor bedroom window in a thunderstorm and was struck again. This knocked his shoes off. Later still, when he was out in the hunting field, lightning struck and hit his dog. Mr. Hobson is buried in Hollywood under a big oak tree, and that tree was struck by lightning too—you can see the mark on the tree. Of course, all this affected Miss Bessie, and whenever there were any thunderstorms, she would shut the windows and get under the chaise in her bedroom.

From time to time, Lord and Lady Astor would come to visit Miss Bessie. Now, Miss Bessie had slate laid out in front of her house as though it was set up for our benefit, so we could play hopscotch. You could throw a rock out to play back and forth. Once, when we were out there playing, Lord Astor came down the front steps, dressed to the nines. Miss Bessie was talking to us along with Lord Astor and Nancy Astor, and I asked him why his nose was so big. Mother and Daddy were completely undone. I had to apologize, of course, and my bicycle, which I had just learned how to ride, was taken away for two weeks. I could not even sit on it. I was very upset, but I learned my lesson: never tell anyone they have a big nose.

When she was there, Lady Astor would come to our house for dinner. She and my maternal grandmother, Gertrude Skelton Hobson, had been very close friends before either one's marriages. They were fierce competitors in the horse world. Of course, they had both ridden sidesaddle and stirred up great excitement in the open jumping classes. At the time, they were considered the top two horsewomen in Virginia. This is probably a strong reason why Lady Astor always dined with us. She referred to us as "Gertrude's poor white trash," which we considered a term of endearment.

One night, sitting across the table from me and participating in a discussion on horses and riding, Lady Astor invited me to come to England to ride her horses and stay for a while. We all thought that was just great. Then Daddy asked, "And where would Trudy stay?" Lady Astor replied, "In the stable of course." The conversation about horses quickly died down. Another night, she decided I would make a perfect wife for her son, Bobby. She jumped up from the dining room table and walked quickly into the kitchen, where there was an old-fashioned black phone attached to the wall. She called her son in New York and excitedly told him that she had found him a bride, her dear friend Gertrude's older granddaughter. I don't know what his comment was, but she hung up the phone, looking dejected. Apparently, she was not aware that he might have been gay.

Joan Lipford was the youngest of three girls and our constant playmate. Her family had moved into 2320 Monument after Mrs. T.A. Cary died, and Miss Cammie Cary moved in with the Cecils. The house was large and wide, with a lovely serpentine brick wall in the back that surrounded a stunning garden in which we never played—it was too beautifully manicured. Hobert Cheatham, called "Hobie" by us, an important member of the Lipford household, ran the show. He was chauffeur, cook, cleaner, ironer, gardener and babysitter for us street urchins, always keeping a watchful eye on us though we didn't know that. (Later in life, Betty, the youngest of his three daughters, tall, polite, circumspect and stylish, came to help me when my daughter was living in Louisville and I lived at English Village on Grove Avenue. I knew her husband, Kenneth Prince, who worked at English Village. He decided his wife could help me. During her first hour, after he dropped her off, while we were cleaning and chatting, I casually mentioned growing up on Monument. She said her father had helped a family on Monument Avenue. "Who?" I asked. "The Lipfords," she responded. "Hobie!" I exclaimed. And then we were off and running. The circle had closed a generation later.)

Weezie Bunnell, another friend, and my oldest in years of knowing each other, lived two blocks east of us. One of my favorite memories was walking to Weezie's house and playing there for the day. Weezie and I had been in the same kindergarten class at Collegiate School in the 1600 block of Monument. We did a lot of roller skating up and down the block, and that's where I learned to ride my two-wheeler. By the time I got to the Lipford house, which was between our house and the Cecil house, I caught on to riding without Daddy holding on to the seat. Somehow, I thought he was still holding on to the seat—a great feeling of security—and off I went.

When we were older, Weezie would often come to our house, and I remember we (Weezie, Berta and I) would get on the cannon in the middle of the grassplot, sit astride it and pretend to shoot down Studebakers. I'm not sure why, but red ones gave you extra points. Berta and I used to bicycle all the way from our house to the Prestwould Apartments, across from Monroe Park, to visit our grandmother, which we thought was very exciting. She was Helen Hamilton Bryan and grew up in Petersburg. Alexander Hamilton was her father, and she married Thomas Pinckney Bryan, our grandfather, who died when my father was about twelve, so of course we never knew him. He was the youngest of five boys and had an older brother, Dr. Robert C. Bryan, who also lived on our block at 2312 Monument, next door to the Cecils.

Uncle Bob had been a surgeon but developed crippling arthritis in both hands and had to wear two rigid paddles strapped to his fingers. I would throw the tennis ball, and he would try to catch it but couldn't, not very well. Brave soul. He would say, "Do it again. Do it again."

Uncle Bob married Grace Hamilton (no relation) from Baltimore, and they had two sons. The younger one, named Bobby, was blond, good-looking, artistic and abhorred violence. He joined the British Ambulance Service before America entered World War II. I remember sitting on the stone steps leading to the front porch from the side yard, posing for him to paint my portrait. I had a mammoth crush on him and didn't mind being very still, as he asked, just to please him. Then he was gone. Bobby was killed on May 17, 1944, in Italy at the crossing of the Rapido River while removing bodies and the wounded from the battlefield. He belonged then to the American Field Service and was buried in Nettuno, Italy, in the American cemetery. Aunt Grace gave me my unfinished portrait, which I still have, plus some stage sets and costume designs constructed for Shakespeare plays.

Bobby Daniel, who lived with his parents at Brandon Plantation in Charles City County, came to stay with Aunt Grace along with his nurse, Cunny, during the war, so he could continue to go to St. Christopher's school. Because of gas rationing, there wouldn't have been enough gas for the Daniels to drive him to Richmond and back every day. Bobby was one of our favorite playmates, and he enthusiastically participated in our escapades up and down the block. I particularly remember going to Bobby's room on the third floor of number 2312 and standing very quietly by his desk, watching him paint his model planes. He did exquisite work, and I was not allowed to touch anything. He was the "boss," although he was a few years younger than me. One time, I did reach out for the treasured gold paint that he was meticulously using on his pilots' goggles. Oh boy. I didn't do that again. The silver paint was off-limits too. I don't remember the connection between Daniel and Aunt Grace, but they were family.

On many Saturdays, my cousin, Anne Hobson, later a nationally recognized author and married to George C. Freeman Jr., would come to play. She wore a wool coat, and her legs were *exposed*. I was swathed either in a snowsuit or a coat with leggings. I asked Anne why she didn't have anything on her legs like me. She was tall, much bigger than I was, and drew herself up, with an air of mighty importance, replying, "Because I am older." Indeed, she was—all of eight months. Oh, mortification. I could not get Mother to relent and let me go barelegged when Anne came to play. I suffered—oh how I suffered. Anne and I have laughed over this incident in our old age. I loved her then as now.

Berta and I played baseball with our father on the grassplot in front of our house. He would throw the ball, and we would catch, or he would pop it with a bat and we'd catch it. Daddy had been boxing captain and assistant coach at the University of Virginia in 1932 while attending law school. It falls to reason that he wanted to teach us boxing, his beloved sport, so he got us boxing gloves, which I still have tucked away in my living room bookcase, among other treasures, all tattered and torn alongside one of Daddy's little boxing statue figures. He started us off on the sidewalk and the living room, and when we got older, he shifted us to shadow boxing in the dining room. I suspect he wanted to make sure we were tough and could take care of ourselves. Daddy would actually hit us—gentle little taps—while we were in training, and Mother would say, "Oh Ham, oh Ham, you are going to kill our daughters." Of course, we responded, "It doesn't hurt, Momma," and it didn't.

Instead of showing movies or puppet shows at my birthday parties, Daddy would rope off the front hall and hold boxing matches, my guest boxers versus his champion (me). Then at one party came the moment of reckoning: the title match featuring Helen Turner, now married to Tayloe Murphy and living in Mount Holly, Virginia, and Trudy Bryan. Helen pinned me against the front door with flying piston fists. She won. Daddy was disgusted with my lack of performance after all his training—up on the toes, bobbing, weaving and deflecting blows. No more boxing birthday parties—a sad afternoon in the Bryan household.

But we had special outings with Daddy. He would take us to the barbershop next to the William Byrd Hotel when he was going to get a haircut. Once, he decided we would get our hair cut too. So the barber put each of us in a chair and shaved the back of our hair up in the 1940s style. He did leave a lock in front of each ear. When Mother saw us, she cried, "Oh Ham, oh Ham, what have you done to our girls?" He would say, "They're alright. They'll be cool for the summer." Sometimes he took us to the Dick Tracy movies at the Capitol Theatre across from Broad Street Station. Scarface scared Berta nearly to death, with lots of tears and nightmares, so we learned quickly to find out if Scarface was a character in the show before we walked to the theater. One Halloween night, Daddy took Berta and me to the Branch House just catty-corner from our block on the southwest corner of Davis Avenue. Standing there in our costumes, we rang the bell and waited and waited. Suddenly, the door flew open, and the chauffeur appeared in his uniform with a pitchfork. He scraped it on the courtyard flagstones, and sparks flew out. We squealed and ran. He scared us to death! Daddy just chuckled.

We had a huge fig tree in the backyard, and I often hid high up in it so I wouldn't have to practice the piano. Mother was a beautiful, talented pianist, and my behavior was very distressful to her. But there was too much to do outside besides playing prisoner to the piano. For example, we raised a lot of puppies in a wired pen underneath the apartment over the garage. There was a little fence around the grassy area where Berta and I had a swing set. Many hours were spent in that small backyard with the puppies and swing set, plotting our daily adventures up and down the block.

We had ducks, two named Dandelion and Daffodil, and we took them for parades down the sidewalk with a string around their necks as a leash. We would go from one end of the block to the other with the ducks, the mother duck in front and the babies just paddling along behind. We also had guinea pigs: Molasses Taffy, Chocolate Fudge and Peppermint Stick, who was white. One of them ran down a rat hole, never to be seen again. We also had kittens of course. They kept coming and coming. It was a wonderful way to learn about "birthin'," and we also learned a lot from Jane Cecil, who was the cat queen. She seemed to have so much cat sense. We loved playing with her kittens, Topsy, Turvy and Midnight; I've never forgotten them to this day.

When I pushed my kittens in their baby carriage, I would wear my Women Accepted for Volunteer Emergency Service (WAVE) uniform, identical to ones women wore in the U.S. Navy. It consisted of a navy blue skirt and jacket with a belt, ribbons, a gold U.S. pin and an anchor pin, a white shirt and a navy blue tie topped off with white bobby socks and brown and white saddle shoes. I felt very proud.

One of our favorite things to do was play with our dolls. They were always getting sick and needed to be nursed and fed day and night. We were constantly giving them bottles of water, changing diapers, rocking them, putting cold, wet washrags on their heads, taking their temperature and loving them. They were loved with such intensity that the paint faded on their faces. Even when we took afternoon walks toward the Lee monument, I would get homesick for my dolls and begged to go home to care for them.

Another favorite pastime for Berta and me was to ride our bikes to Broad Street Station to watch the trains come and go. The station was cavernous, with a model train in the large waiting room. This is also where we would find the latest comic books. The drugstore on Addison Street had comics too, as well as pink bubble gum balls with comic wrappers. With our quarter allowance, we would decide how many pieces of penny gum we could buy after purchasing our comic books at ten cents each. Between the two of us, with fifty cents at the ready, we could do some maneuvering. The trick was to read as many as we could while in the drugstore and then take one or two home to devour.

Growing up without television (although we did have a radio), we relied on our imaginations. When the weather was nice, we always played outside.

At worst, Berta and I would lie on our stomachs on the upstairs front porch and toss little balloons filled with water over the side and try to hit Mr. and Mrs. Gay taking their afternoon stroll on the sidewalk. A more imaginative game was playing "Sheena," the jungle girl, and "Wonder Woman" in our bathing suits, galoshes (magic boots), towels attached to our shoulders as capes and a shortened clothesline for her magic lasso. We learned to climb and walk all the backyard walls, those between houses and along the alley of our block, without touching the ground. We thought we were pretty spectacular and *shazammed* all over the place. It was lucky we weren't killed.

I remember coming home from school; we would have caught the bus, gotten off to transfer to the streetcar and ridden it to Robinson and Monument. We would walk across the street, and there we would always find Mr. Louis Held. He lived in the yellow apartments, sat on the porch and handed out ladyfingers. He always had ladyfingers. We didn't like them, but he was so excited to give them to us that we took them. Our hands were already dirty, so by the time we got back to number 2326, the ladyfingers were black with dirt so we could only eat one end.

In our family, we had Gladys Ross and Fannie Mae Hopkins to take care of us. Gladys lived in Goochland near the Crozier Road, and Fannie lived out on Gaskins Road in Henrico County. But they had a small apartment on top of the garage behind our house to which they could escape. Gladys took care of the downstairs and cooked. Fannie Mae was in charge of upstairs, ironed and tended to Berta and me. She saw to our baths, got us up for school and made sure we ate our breakfast and didn't forget our homework. She was so gentle, soft-spoken and kind. We both loved her. "Miss Berta, don't you treat Miss Trudy like that—now you girls be sweet to each other. You know that ain't no way to act."

Gladys had the most inviting lap, always available for confidences. She had helped our grandmother, Gertrude Skelton Hobson, who managed Tuckahoe Plantation for the Harold Jefferson Coolidge family of Boston, Massachusetts. After Mother's wedding at Tuckahoe Plantation in 1933, Gladys and Fannie Mae moved with our grandmother to Plum Street and lived there until she died. It was then that Gladys and Fanny came to us. They were both rock solid during our growing-up years, teaching us values and the right way to do things. For example, they showed us how to set a table, how to serve on the left and remove from the right and how to serve ourselves when the food was passed. We learned to place our knife and fork in the four o'clock position when we finished eating so Fannie knew we were through and could clear our plates. Gladys even taught me a little cooking, like how

Berta and Trudy Bryan reading with their father, Hamilton Bryan. *Courtesy of Gertrude Skelton Bryan.*

to peel a small white potato, boil it, slather it with butter and sprinkle it with Lawry's Seasoning Salt. Yum. I still do it. But while Gladys was helping me with "learning how to cook," she was mumbling that I was never going to need to learn how to cook. Wasn't Gladys the optimistic one?

Gladys and Mother had a daily ritual. They would collaborate each morning on what to have for supper. Mother would then call the Richmond Grocerteria on Addison Street (now Strawberry Street) and place an order, like "a nice steak, rice or potatoes, and fresh vegetables," which was often spinach. The spinach was served on a platter ringed with grated yellow egg yoke and then an outer ring of grated egg white. It was very pretty when freshly presented, but the picture was drastically altered after Mother took the first helping and ruined the symmetry. I loved the eggs with the spinach, but I never got the first swipe. I was sure I wouldn't mess it up so badly. Sometimes we had asparagus on buttered toast when we were running low on meat coupons during the war, or we had what Mother and Gladys called "Cheese Surprise," which was a slice of tomato hidden under a slice of cheese on top of toast run under the broiler so the cheese puffed up. A favorite breakfast dish at Christmas was scrambled eggs, fresh salted roe herring (the fish having been soaked in water overnight) and batter bread (a little stiffer than spoon bread). Oh what heaven! But the very best was spreading the roe herring like jam on a piece of buttered toast and then topping it off with more butter. Utter bliss. We all loved it.

The grocery boy would arrive in the early afternoon on his bike with whatever had been ordered that morning. The order also included any food and cooking essentials, such as bread, cookies, spices, canned goods and so forth. The Richmond Grocerteria gave us charging privileges, and Mother would go over every single item by phone at the end of the month before paying the bill. We also had a laundry service provided by Don's. The driver would enter the house through the back door, gallop up the back stairs to the second floor to pick up sheets, pillowcases and towels stashed at the top of the steps. That was a Monday ritual, and the bed linens were returned by the end of the week all ironed and folded.

Then there was Mr. Reuben. As others have mentioned, Reuben was everything. He had a delicatessen and sold ice cream, which he packed into paper cartons. My mother would call Reuben's every night, it seemed to me, asking him to send up some ice cream for dessert. So Reuben would pack chocolate ice cream in the paper carton, and the boy who worked for him, Eddie, would bring it up by bicycle in time for dessert. Sometimes we would ride our bicycles down to Park and Meadow and pick up the ice cream, but I was scared of Eddie. He was menacing looking.

On weekends, Gladys brought her grandson, Junie (Junior), and her granddaughter, Vergie Mae, to our house. Junie and I played mother and father, with Vergie as our baby. Junie could make Vergie stop crying, but I had a hard time with this. She seemed to like Junie better than me, and I felt a little bit jealous. Gladys and Fannie were an integral part of our lives. They made our world tick and held us tight. Neither ever raised their voices, but they quietly and surely made their point. They held their ground and we understood. We loved them, knew they loved us and felt so privileged having them in our lives for so many years.

In fact, our lives on Monument were uniquely special. We knew no fear. Our front door was rarely locked. We felt completely free to do whatever we wanted and go wherever. We were given a long, loose rein. We were mobile and didn't need assistance. We had bikes, skates, streetcars and buses. We were hungry for adventure and excitement and made our own. We rarely asked permission but checked in, when we remembered, with Fannie and Gladys. We had a very good life. We felt loved, cradled and abundantly free, and this released our spirits. We soared.

ROBERTA BRYAN BOCOCK

My father and mother were Alexander Hamilton Bryan and Gertrude Hobson Bryan. My sister, Trudy, and I lived at 2326 Monument Avenue. I was born on August 15, 1937, and was really the baby on the block. We lived right across from John Cecil's cannon. When he lit the cannon, I never heard it go off as I was only two and a half months old.

One of my great memories, really a huge part of my life, was going down to the Cecil house. We ran in and out of the house like it was our own. Actually, on our block, we ran in and out of everybody's house, but interestingly enough, mostly east of number 2326. We went west to the Hamilton house to play with Sue Hamilton, and we were in and out of the Donahues' backyard. We ran into Miss Bessie Hobson's at number 2324, the Lipfords' next door to them at number 2320, the Cecils' house and then the Robert Bryans' house. Next came the Laffertys' and Dr. Stuart McGuire's and then, on the corner, the house of Helen Gregory and her baby sister, Anne.

Aunt Grace Bryan's (Mrs. Robert C. Bryan) house, number 2312, looked like a castle on Monument Avenue. Jake and Bobby Bryan grew up there. To the right of the front steps, she had a tall hedge of hemlock trees. Under the trees were beautiful magenta azaleas. An old magnolia tree stood in her side yard, and it was one of the greatest climbing trees on the block. We spent many hours in its branches, dreaming up adventures. Inside the house, a moose head was hung in the den, and we loved being allowed to look at it. Aunt Grace Bryan continued to be a close part of our family and brought happiness to our lives.

Aside from Bobby Daniel, whom my sister has already mentioned, another playmate was Edgar Lafferty. He was much younger, but he joined the team. Mable, his nurse, was one of our keepers. Another friend on our block was Joan Lipford. She was our age and also our partner in crime on our Monument Avenue travels. Hobie was the Lipfords' butler, and Sadie was their cook. Hobie was very kind and soft-spoken. He was a full member of our gang and kept an eagle eye on us in a gentle way. Sadie made us behave and step lively.

In the middle of the Lipfords' beautiful garden was a large silver ball on a pedestal that fascinated me. The first flower I remember seeing, besides the dandelion and buttercup, was a pink Bleeding Heart in that same garden. The plant was next to the east wall between the Lipfords' and the Cecils' houses. I still love this flower, but today, my Bleeding Heart doesn't touch the beauty of Mrs. Lipford's flower. A walled garden must be the perfect location.

One of my happiest memories with the Lipford family was "calling the fairies." Most mornings when we were about four to five years old, I would walk down to the Lipfords' and ring the front door. Mr. Lipford would welcome me and lead me into the living room. There, with other children, I turned around and hid my eyes so that Mr. Lipford could "call the fairies." He would sit down at his grand piano, which had a smaller electric keyboard attached, and play a little trill. The music would call the fairies, and the fairies would leave candy on the keyboard. Afterward, he would tiptoe out the door to his waiting car and go to work. We all knew this was a game, and we loved it.

As we've all been saying, on our block our families turned us loose at a pretty early age. Once we learned to ride our bicycles, we were free to go, and go we did. They gave us all very long leashes. I often rode my bicycle down to the Robert E. Lee monument, where I would meet my friend Mary Blair Scott. From there, we would take off. I don't know if my mother and father taught me this or whether I figured it out on my own, but I always stayed on the sidewalk when I rode my bike, and I always watched the cars beside the sidewalk. If there was a lone person in a car, I stopped right away and would always cross the street to the grassplot and then on to the other side, never passing the car. I really think that was the beginning of street smarts and staying safe.

The major part of my Monument Avenue adventures was going to the Cecils' house. I learned how to train dogs with Pat, who had taught their bull terrier, Bully, to climb the ladder up onto the brick wall around their garden. He would

Berta in dog training class with Pat Cecil's dog, Eric. *Courtesy of Patricia Cecil Hass.*

Berta and Trudy sitting with Blackie-Brownie. *Courtesy of Gertrude Skelton Bryan.*

trot around up there, looking at the alley and barking at the alley cats, and then he would slide back down the sliding board. In those days, all our dogs knew where their houses were, but they also ran around loose, and we thought we should train them to stay out of the street. Sadly, all our efforts didn't work for our cocker spaniel, Blackie-Brownie Bryan, who had almost enough championship points and was going to the Westminster Dog Show. Blackie's trainers were Pat and Jane Cecil, Lindsey Graham and Betty Bowe Wallace. Right before the Westminster show, Blackie-Brownie was hit by a car in front of our house and killed. Our family was so sad, and we never forgot it.

Our block had racing homing pigeons, too. Buddy Donahue, who lived next door to us on the west side, started raising pigeons, and one summer, he showed the Cecils' butler, William, how to build a coop in the backyard. So we all watched the pigeons lay eggs and raise their young, and when they were old enough to race, we would take them in a crate to Broad Street Station and put them on the baggage car of a train going north. Then we'd ask the baggage man to let them loose in Fredericksburg or Washington. The pigeons would race back to Monument Avenue. We pretty much knew when they were going to get there, and we would stand in the garden and wait for them; it was so exciting to watch them come flying in, land on the coop and go inside. It was just so much fun being a part of that whole scene because there was always something exciting going on, especially in the summer, when we were really a gang. I wasn't old enough to do everything, but the older children took me with them, and I took it all in, always.

We would always wait for the Richmond Dairy milk wagon to come up the alley. A horse pulled it, and the girls thought the man who drove it was so cute. He gave me Dentyne chewing gum, and we would always just wait for him to come. His name was Tom Sawyer—that was his real name. He had blue eyes and black hair, and Pat thought he was very good-looking, but I don't remember looking at him. I just remember playing with the horse. Everyone grew fig trees up and down Monument Avenue on the north side of their houses. Some of those fig trees are still there. We would go up and down the alley into people's yards, pick figs and take them around to neighbors.

Billy Hill wrote about jumping across the rooftops on Park Avenue. We did the same thing on our block, but not from roof to roof. We would start at Addison Street, and we could go all the way down the block toward Davis Avenue on fences and garages and never touch the ground. We actually got to the Hamiltons' house, but we never went to the Sneads' house. One day, we jumped down into Dr. Stuart McGuire's big brick areaway. I said if we got down there, we could get out. Well, of course, we couldn't get out

Dr. Stuart McGuire's house on the 2300 block of Monument. *Courtesy of the Valentine Richmond History Center.*

Number 2315 Monument Avenue, Eleanor Barton's house; the walled garden was called "Emerald City." *Courtesy of Roberta Bryan Bocock.*

because it was a ten-foot wall of bricks. So they called the fire department, and the firemen lowered a ladder so that we could climb out. Dr. and Mrs. McGuire were really patient about it all.

"Emerald City" was what we called our secret world across the street. There was an empty lot next door to the Barton house. No one took care of the lot, and the weedy grass was about three feet tall. We crossed Monument Avenue with garden shears, stepping over the tall weeds as best we could so no one would see our trail from the curbing and sidewalk. Carefully, we clipped a narrow path to the middle of the lot and cut out a round section so we could sit down in our hideout. Completely hidden from the street, we drank our Royal Crown (RC) Colas. No one could possibly know our hideout, and to us it was another Monument Avenue secret.

When I was eleven years old and in sixth grade, my father and I studied Latin every Friday night. Our book was *Latin Book One*, by Scott Forsman and Company (1936). He prepared each lesson, and we worked them out together. With no pressure, I had time to master each lesson and solve the puzzle of the proper ending for each word plus make up vocabulary cards so that I could memorize the words. Best of all, seventh-grade Latin was easy, as I had already studied from the Latin book.

After our study hall, the real fun started. My father, my cocker spaniel, Beau, and I would walk around the block to Davis Avenue and Broad Street to the New England Grill, owned by Mike. There we would watch the Friday night boxing matches on TV. Television was brand new in my life. As we didn't have a TV, this was an unbelievable treat. My father always had a beer, and I drank Tru Ades, an orange drink. We watched lots of famous boxing matches with Joe Louis, Sugar Ray Robinson, Rocky Graziano and Ezzard Charles. We sat at the bar, with Beau lying under my barstool. One Friday night, a customer tried to pat Beau, but he would have none of it. Beau tried to bite him but didn't succeed. I'll never forget the terrifying noise under my barstool.

Gillette Blue Blades was the commercial for the Friday night fights, and I loved to sing along with the popular Gillette Blue Blades Marching Song. The jingle goes this way:

> *To Look sharp every time you shave,*
> *To Feel sharp and be on the ball,*
> *To Be sharp, use Gillette Blue Blades,*
> *It's the quickest, slickest shave of all.*

I loved my Friday nights with my father, and I loved a story I remember about him and Lady Astor (Nancy Langhorne Astor). As my sister has said, she would visit often, as she was a great friend of Miss Bessie's. Miss Bessie, Marie and Madelyn would make us "step lively" and clean up the yard. As we had many pets, they encouraged us to do an extra special good job, and we did.

One evening, when I was around ten or eleven years old, Lady Astor was visiting Miss Bessie, and we invited them to dinner. All of us "put on the dog" for Lady Astor. She had such a quick wit. She could ask a question and answer it before you even started to think of the answer. My father was seated at the end of the table. Lady Astor was on his left, and I was on his right. While Lady Astor was talking to Mother at the other end of the table, my father stole the butter ball off Lady Astor's butter plate. As I held my breath, I saw it happen in slow motion and wondered what in the world she would do. In a flash, she stole the butter ball back with great fanfare while she chatted away. We all had a good laugh. My father almost succeeded.

When Jake Bryan came home from World War II, I waited outside Aunt Grace's house sitting on the front steps, and he drove up in a taxicab. I remember thinking that this was an incredible time, especially since his younger brother, Bobby, who served as an ambulance driver with the American Field Service, had been killed. That was in 1946, and also that year, Winston Churchill and General Dwight Eisenhower came to Richmond. Churchill was to make a speech on the steps of the Capitol Square. For some reason, St. Catherine's School did not schedule a holiday so that we could go to the square to hear the speech, but our mother took my sister and me out of school anyway. At the appointed time, Miss Bessie Hobson, our next-door neighbor, Mother, Trudy and I walked across Monument Avenue to the grassplot and awaited the parade. Gerry Bemiss's father, Mr. Sam Bemiss, had provided his big, beautiful green convertible for the two heroes, so we knew we would really see them. When they passed by us, Miss Bessie said in a loud voice, "Look at that baby face." I thought that was the oddest remark, but now I know what she meant. After the parade went by, we hurried back across the street and got in our car, a black Ford, nicknamed Pearl Harbor. Miss Bessie did not join us. Mother drove east through the alleys of Richmond as far as she could, and then we walked to the Capitol Square to hear Churchill. I knew this was a famous day in my life.

As a side note, my future mother-in-law, Elisabeth Scott Bocock, also walked from her house at 909 West Franklin Street to the Capital Square to hear Churchill's speech. Always a creative person with real style, she was armed with a silver champagne cooler filled with a bottle of iced-down vintage champagne to give to Churchill. Tied to the cooler was a note to Churchill with a return address, thanking him for all he had done for our country and the world during World War II. She managed to position herself at the front of the crowd next to the rope that everyone stood behind. At the proper moment, when Churchill came to the podium, she shot under the rope holding the champagne cooler and hurriedly walked toward the podium where Churchill was standing. Of course, security met her in full force, and she gave them the cooler. Then she returned to her place and ducked back under the rope to await Churchill's speech. The next day, the champagne cooler was returned to her house, with a thank-you note from Mr. Churchill. I have never seen the note, but what an adventure for all!

Eleanor Barton and her sister, Edith, and brother, Bobby, lived across from us at 2315 Monument. The house was a tall Spanish structure built by Mr. and Mrs. Scott Parrish, Eleanor Barton's grandfather and grandmother. Scott Parrish's daughter, Eleanor Parrish, married Robert Barton. Of their three children, Edith married Reverend Charles Sheerin of Woodberry Forest School, and Bobby Barton started a ski area in Davis, West Virginia. Eleanor Barton was our age and our friend.

The Churchill and Eisenhower parade arrives in Capital Square, with the John Marshall High School band in the background. *Courtesy of the Valentine Richmond History Center.*

Charles Gillette, the landscape architect, was Scott Parrish's close friend. Mr. Gillette designed small, thin, rectangular ponds in the side entrance to the house. The back garden had a long pond divided into three sections. You could jump across these ponds, or on hot days, we would wade in them. After a while, the maid, the cook or the butler would come out and make us get out because we were disturbing the goldfish. Eleanor's dog, Wren, was part boxer, black with white on his chest and floppy ears. We taught him how to play hide-and-seek all through the Barton house. The living room, facing Monument Avenue, had the most hiding places. Wren caught on right away and was so joyful when he found us. Mrs. Parrish was very patient and our friend as well. She let us have the run of the house, especially on rainy days. The ballroom was on the third floor and was great fun to play in, racing back and forth across the huge space.

Eleanor Barton and William Button's wedding was in the fall of 1957 at Eleanor's house, 2315 Monument Avenue, across the street from my house.

Berta Bryan (Bocock) on Roman Soldier, 1952. *Courtesy of Gertrude Skelton Bryan.*

I met my future husband, Freddy Bocock, at her wedding. I remember that I was wearing an emerald green dress and peacock blue shoes. Neither Freddy nor I liked to stand in long receiving lines, and I was quick to jump the receiving line with a plan to swing back through it when it wasn't so long.

Apparently, Freddy had the same idea. We met at the back of the tent on the side yard. As we were trying to crawl under the tent, Walter Glenn, the bartender and my friend, lifted up the tent and said, "Hello, Mr. Bocock. Hello, Miss Bryan." We all laughed and met one another, and somehow Freddy and I continued to talk when we actually got to the reception. I remember it was mostly about horses, as we were both riders. He asked me if he could take me riding the next day, a Sunday, and our courtship progressed from there. But of course, it started where everything started for me, on Monument Avenue.

In 1963, throughout the spring, summer and fall, Richmond was in a huge drought. In early October, Nancy Lancaster, Lady Astor's niece, came to visit Miss Bessie Hobson. We liked to watch her "do the Hucklebuck" on the sidewalk in front of Miss Bessie's house. Nancy always stayed on the third floor. She loved to dance. While staying with us, she danced around a lot, doing high kicks. All of us thought that between the plaster drying out from the drought and Nancy dancing on the third floor, it caused the ceiling to fall, which happened at the end of October, around Halloween. Miss Bessie was on the chaise after lunch watching TV, which she loved to do, when suddenly the ceiling slowly started peeling down on top of her. She slid down in the chaise, and the tall piece of furniture, called a highboy, on which she kept her hats, caught the ceiling and made a cave. Madelyn Walker, her housekeeper, heard the noise, came upstairs, looked in the room and saw the ceiling totally dropped down on the chaise and Miss Bessie. Miss Bessie said she heard Madelyn say, "Jeeeesus." Then Madelyn called the fire department. When the firemen arrived, they climbed a ladder to the second floor and came in the front window facing Monument Avenue. It was the only way they could get in the room and lift the ceiling off Miss Bessie. Off she went down the front steps on a stretcher, even though she was not hurt at all, and she was furious that they insisted on taking her to Stuart Circle Hospital. Dr. Jimmy Dalton took care of her.

While she was there, I went to see her and said, "Please save your room for me because my baby is about to be born and I want this room." Jack Bocock, my second child, was born two weeks later on November 14, 1963, and that was the room I got. The Monument Avenue continuity was complete.

The people who worked for our families were actually like an extended family for all of the gang of children on our block, and certainly they were an integral part of our Monument Avenue adventures. Fannie Mae Smith Hopkins lived on Gaskins Road in Henrico County; Gladys Ross and Elise Wall were from Crozier, Virginia; and Madelyn Walker and William and Marie Montague were from Richmond, Virginia.

Fannie Mae, her four brothers—Leslie, Peter, Philip and Thomas—and her mother, Carrie Smith, lived at Tuckahoe Plantation, just west of Richmond off River Road. My grandparents, Corydon and Gertrude Hobson, managed that plantation for Harold Jefferson Coolidge of Boston, Massachusetts. In 1942, Fannie came to my family on Monument Avenue to take care of my sister, Trudy, and me. She soon became my soul mate.

She was my nurse but, more importantly, my teacher. Her lessons covered how to tie my shoes, bathe my cocker spaniel, Beau, in my bathtub and clean up all the mess, polish my brown and white saddle shoes and clean their rubber soles. She was a natural nurse with a genuine talent for quietly accomplishing the goals she set for herself. She would control me as Dr. Emily Gardner gave me my summer camp shots (the dreaded stinging tick fever shot), nursed me through red measles and chicken pox and, most of all, took care of all my battle wounds from running the streets.

When Freddy Bocock and I married in September 1959, Fannie became a part of our family in 1967 and helped to raise our four children. Freddy and I realized how blessed we were to have her teaching them the same basic lessons she'd taught me. She lived her final days at the Westminster-Canterbury Health Care Center. She died in January 1986 and is buried in the cemetery on Quioccasin Road. Her gravestone has a lamb carved on it, as she was as kind and gentle as a lamb.

Our family's other helper was Gladys Ross, who had also worked for my grandparents at Tuckahoe Plantation. She came to my family on Monument Avenue in about 1944 to be our family cook. Her cooking was so tasty—shad roe, oyster soup, spot fish, roe herring and batterbread were my favorites. Her custard dessert, "Floating Island," was unbeatable.

She was a jovial friend, always full of laughter and on to all our tricks, like hiding food we didn't like behind the radiator. She never scolded us. She taught me how to boil water and other basic cooking at an early age. During World War II, butter, maple syrup and brown sugar were scarce or nonexistent as they all went to the war effort. I was allowed to knead the yellow color into the margarine to make it look like butter for the rolls. There were so many tricks to making food taste good as we waited out the war. Gladys was a caring, loyal friend, and all of our family loved her for the happiness and peace she brought into our lives. She came to my own family in 1982. Once again, Fannie and Gladys were a part of raising my four children and being an anchor in my life. Gladys died on August 4, 1989, and is buried beside her husband, Richard Ross, at First Union Baptist Church in Crozier, Virginia.

For years, Elise Wall would come to our family to do ironing. She was very calm, and I loved working with her to learn how to iron. Under her supervision, I was allowed to iron napkins and pillowcases. The reward was instant results. Elise also lived in Crozier, which is about forty minutes west of Richmond, so it was a long commute for them.

Marie Montague and Madelyn Walker worked for Miss Bessie Hobson at number 2324. They were our next-door neighbors and tolerated our adventuresome ideas. At the same time, they made us mind and have manners. Marie and her husband, William, lived over Miss Bessie's garage, and Madelyn lived on Montrose Street on the north side of Richmond. They kept up with us as we climbed the fences and stocked our clubhouse

Miss Bessie Hobson (Mrs. Saunders Hobson) holding Natalie Bocock, the winter of 1961. *Courtesy of Roberta Bryan Bocock.*

under the side porch with chairs and Ritz crackers and cheese. All our food brought on rats. That was the end of our clubhouse.

Marie was famous for her light bread rolls. When she started baking, the tantalizing aroma would float over the backyard fence. I would make a dash for Miss Bessie's front door bell and ring the bell. Knowing that Marie would leave the kitchen and answer the front door, I would run around to the kitchen door, dart in, grab a few cooling rolls and run out the back door. She must have known my trick but never let on nor locked the kitchen door. Marie and Madelyn were as much a part of my life as Fannie Mae and Gladys.

The most rewarding part of writing our Monument Avenue memories is reading my other friends' stories in this book. Each of us knew that we were totally original in our adventures, but we were not! It became clear that children moving in a troop in the same environment of grassplots, sidewalks for bicycling and roller skating, backyard fences and roofs to climb around on and side lots to play in would create the same imagination. We could roam around Monument Avenue and entertain ourselves for hours. Our lives were filled with independence and freedom to try all our ideas, and we were allowed at a young age to ride streetcars and buses around the city. Monument Avenue was magical for all of us.

HENRY HARRISON WILSON JR.

When my father died near the end of May 1933, I was one month less than ten years of age. At that time, my family and I lived in Harrisburg, Pennsylvania. My mother, a native of Pulaski County, Virginia, and subsequently a resident of Radford and Richmond, announced to me, my brother, Tyler, and my sister, Lily, that our family would soon be leaving Harrisburg to live in Richmond. My father's funeral service in June 1933 commenced at the home of our cousins in Ginter Park, the Richard C. Wight family, and ended at Hollywood Cemetery. Our family spent the summer of 1933 in Radford, and in September, we began our residency at 2340 Monument Avenue.

My cousin, John Howe Cecil Jr., lived on the same block, at number 2314. Very fortunately for me, John was the proud possessor of an intriguing Lionel O-gauge electric train. At that point, my own train was an "ancient" Standard-gauge train inherited from my brother, Tyler. Due to the kindness of John Cecil and his family, I spent far more time in the fall of 1933 playing with John's train than with mine. All of this occurred during the height of the Great Depression, and my mother prepared me for a modest 1933 Christmas. To my considerable surprise, when Christmas arrived, I opened package after package and found a brand-new set of the then-latest Hiawatha Lionel train. I think John Cecil was a little bit envious of me—quite a reversal! But of course, I shared; he came to play at our house.

Another matter of interest to me in those days was the considerable attention a number of our friends expressed about the family car that we arrived in when we moved to Richmond from Harrisburg. My father had bought the car when he attended a business convention in Philadelphia a year or two before his death. It was a DuPont limousine, and the engine was basically aluminum rather than the usual steel. The headlights were unique—very narrow, probably two and a half to three inches wide from top to bottom, with a height of probably ten and a half inches. There were folding seats immediately behind the chauffeur's front seat and in front of the primary rear seat. The windows in the rear compartment of the automobile were fitted with individual curtains. I believe that nearly everyone we knew assumed that my mother was a multimillion-dollar heiress, but unfortunately that was not so. She sold the car after we had lived on Monument Avenue for a year or so, and the automobile dealer who sold my mother a Graham Paige car told us that the DuPont engine that had been removed was being used for power in a sawmill outside Richmond.

While living on Monument Avenue, I was introduced to the art of carpooling, which was carried out by Cecils, the Gayles from Park Avenue and the Wilsons. Douglas Swink, who lived about two blocks west of the 2300 block, did not participate in our carpool and was taken regularly to St. Christopher's School in his family's red Lincoln sedan. He always sat on the rear seat, in the middle, with his red hair showing through the rear window of the car. It was a picture that has been etched in my brain for many years.

When our tenancy at number 2340 ended after about two and a half years, my mother moved her residency to the family home she had inherited from her parents in Radford.

COLEMAN WORTHAM III

Number 2301 Monument Avenue has a unique history. Built by my grandparents, Mr. and Mrs. Coleman Wortham, it is the only house that has never left its original family. The house was commissioned in 1914, but the First World War interrupted its construction. The interim allowed for some changes to the original plan, and it was finally completed in 1926, the first Richmond commission for William Lawrence Bottomley and the beginning of his reign as a favored architect of elegant houses all over Richmond, five of which joined number 2301 on that same 2300 block.

My grandparents moved into the home in 1926 with their son and two daughters, and sadly, my grandfather had only six years in his house, dying in 1932. My grandmother stayed on with my father, Coleman Wortham Jr., and his two sisters, Nancy and Mary Hoge. Eventually, my father and my Aunt Mary Hoge married and set up their own households, but Nancy stayed to take care of my grandmother.

However, in 1951, Nancy, now in her forties, declared that she was going to marry Mr. Sam Jackson, to our family's surprise and delight. This meant that she would no longer be running her bedridden mother's household, and she announced that it was my father's turn to take over my grandmother's care. So, my father and mother and my sister and I came back to live at number 2301. At that time, my sister and I were the only young children on the block. We never played on the median; by that time, there were too many cars. Our friends lived "in the fan"—on Park Avenue, the street behind our house, or on Stuart or Hanover or West Avenues. We mostly

Number 2301 Monument Avenue. The Coleman Wortham III house has stayed continuously in the Wortham family. *Courtesy of the Valentine Richmond History Center.*

played in the triangle park at Meadow Street and Park Avenue, or on West Avenue, affectionately known as "Stork Alley" for obvious reasons. People who lived on West Avenue, then as now, considered the street their common living room. I traveled up and down from number 2301 to West Avenue by way of the alleys, which were much safer than the streets, prettier and more interesting as well.

When we arrived, my grandmother had 'round-the-clock nurses and a fairly large household staff, but my mother slowly reduced the staff down to Carolyn Taylor, who remained with my mother and then my family until she retired in 2010, and Ossi, the butler. Occasionally, my mother would ask Ossi to walk down to pick up my sister, Anne, from the Collegiate school, which in the 1950s was still on Monument Avenue. Ossi was a very formal butler who became extremely agitated if mother did not give him appropriate warning so he could don his morning coat. My little sister was often seen walking up Monument Avenue hand in hand with this tall, elegant, dignified member of our family. This same scene repeated itself in the 1990s, when Carolyn Taylor would walk to pick up my children from First Baptist Church preschool at the corner of Monument and the Boulevard. I will never forget seeing Carolyn walking down the street with my son, Coleman, bouncing the ball back and forth between them. Our lives were immeasurably enriched by these wonderful friends.

During the 1950s and '60s, Monument Avenue lost some of its glow as the houses were turned into apartments and offices or fell into disrepair. My father died in 1963, and my mother put the house in my name. Determined that we would stay there, she bought the distinguished gift shop E.B. Taylor in 1964, as well as its relative, the Hampton House, a few years later. My sister and I lived at number 2301 through college. I married my wife, Lindsay, in 1976, and we turned the garage into a carriage house and lived there for seven years. When my mother became ill in 1988, we moved into the big house with our daughter and son. They were the fourth generation raised at 2301 Monument Avenue.

It has been wonderful to see Monument Avenue return to its former glory as new young families with children have moved into the big houses and professionals have recognized the beauty hidden behind apartment walls or office partitions and restored these gems to their original splendor. I feel so lucky to have been able to live my whole life in this beautiful house on this magnificent street, and I look forward to one of my children being able to say the same. It only takes one drive down Monument Avenue at night at Christmastime to see that Monument Avenue, too, has been reborn.

APPENDIX

W e, the authors, have added the following gallery of images, which we hope portrays the era and some of our houses with their surroundings on the blocks we inhabited. This may in some measure convey a feeling for the time and architecture, if not for the life we lived moving around in that architecture. That, hopefully, we have described in our preceding stories.

Miss Bessie Hobson and Trudy and Berta Bryan's helpers. *Left to right*: Marie Montague, Gladys Ross, Elise Wall, Fannie Mae Hopkins and Madelyn Walker. *Courtesy of Roberta Bryan (Bocock).*

Above: The wedding of Mary Hill and Harry Bishop at 1810 Monument Avenue, 1938. *Courtesy of William M. Hill.*

Left: Miss Traylor's Ballet.

North side of the 2300 block. *Left to right*: 2330 Monument Avenue, Donahue House; 2326 Monument Avenue, Roberta Bryan Bocock; and 2324 Monument Avenue, Miss Bessie Hobson. *Courtesy of Roberta Bryan Bocock.*

Number 2320 Monument Avenue. Mrs. T.A. Cary, later Walter Lipford; 2314 Monument Avenue, Mr. and Mrs. John Howe Cecil; and 2312 Monument Avenue, Dr. and Mrs. Robert Bryan. *Courtesy of Roberta Bryan Bocock.*

Anne Willson Harrison (Eastman's) house at 2023 Monument Avenue. *Courtesy of the Valentine Richmond History Center.*

Number 2020 Monument Avenue. *Courtesy of Archer Christian Burke.*

Number 1810 Monument Avenue. *Courtesy of William Maury Hill.*

Number 1811 Monument Avenue. *Courtesy of Susan Ewing.*

NOTES ON SOURCES

Most of the information in the foreword came from three books:

Driggs, Sarah Shields, Richard Guy Wilson and Robert P. Winthrop. *Richmond's Monument Avenue.* 2nd ed. Chapel Hill: University of North Carolina Press, 2001.

Edwards, Kathy, Esme Howard and Toni Prawl. *Monument Avenue: History and Architecture.* Washington, D.C.: U.S. Department of the Interior, National Park Service, Cultural Resources, HABS/HAER, 1992.

Scott, Mary Wingfield. *Old Richmond Neighborhoods.* Richmond, VA: Whittet and Shepperson, 1950.

The quotes (with the exception of the story at the end) are taken from *Richmond's Monument Avenue.*

ABOUT THE EDITOR

Patricia Hass spent her childhood on Richmond's famed Monument Avenue. She is an editor-at-large with Alfred A. Knopf. She has edited titles by four Supreme Court justices, a president, a secretary of state and many others throughout her illustrious career. She makes her home in Washington, D.C.

CPSIA information can be obtained
at www.ICGtesting.com
Printed in the USA
LVHW080003150620
658072LV00009B/173